Liar: The Truth About Lies and the People Who Tell Them

by R. Johnson

© 2012, Michael Anderson. All rights reserved.

This book contains material protected under International and Federal Copyright Laws and Treaties. Any unauthorized reprint or use of this material is prohibited. No part of this book may be reproduced or transmitted in any form or by any means, electronic or mechanical, including photocopying, recording, or by any information storage and retrieval system without express written permission from the author.

Disclaimer:

The information contained in this book is for general information purposes only. This book is sold with the understanding the author and/or publisher is not giving medical advice, nor should this book replace medical advice, nor is it intended to diagnose or treat any disease, illness or other medical condition.

This book is a nonfiction book. However, the names and characteristics of the individuals in the book, as well as some of the events, have been fictionalized in order to protect the identities of the people contained herein. Any semblance to a person living or dead is incidental and unintentional.

While we endeavor to keep the information up to date and correct, we make no representations or warranties of any kind, express or implied, about the completeness, accuracy, reliability, suitability or availability with respect to the book or the information, products, services, or related graphics contained book for any purpose. Any reliance you place on such information is therefore strictly at your own risk.

In no event will we be liable for any liability, loss or damage including without limitation, indirect or consequential loss or damage, or any loss or damage whatsoever arising from loss of data or profits arising out of, or in connection with, the use of the material or the interpretation of the material contained in this book.

Dedication:

This book is dedicated to all the honest people out there. I hope you find something in here to help you fight the forces of evil . . . or at least to help you tell when you're being deceived.

Contents

Preface 7
Chapter 1: Types of Lies 9
   1.1: White Lies 14
   1.2: Ethical Lies 16
   1.3: Lying By Omission 19
   1.4: Bold-Faced Lie 22
   1.5: Fabrications 24
   1.6: Secondary Lies 26
   1.7: Denial 28
   1.8: Minimization 30
Chapter 2: Types of Liars 32
   2.1: The Pathological Liar 34
   2.2: The Opportunistic Liar 38
   2.3: The Unskilled Liar 40
   2.4: The Smooth Operator 42
   2.5: The Sociopathic Liar 43
   2.6: The Polite Liar 45
Chapter 3: How to Protect Yourself from Lies 46
   3.1: The Truth Bias 49
   3.2: Honing Your Deception Detection Skills 52
      1: Does this sound too good to be true? 56

2: What do I know of the person making the statement? 56

3: Are there parts of what you're being told that don't ring true? 57

4: What does this person have to gain by lying? 58

5: Is there a way for me to verify whether the statement is true or false?.. 59

6: If I were listening to this person make this statement to someone else, would I believe it to be true? 61

7: What is the cost to me (or others I care about) if this is a lie? 61

3.3: Watch What They Say 62

3.4: Identifying an Online Liar.. 68

The Online Dating Dilemma.. 75

Chapter 4: The Best Defense against Lies and Those Who Tell Them.. 80

4.1: The Only Way You Can Be Lied to Is If You Let it Happen 82

Chapter 5: The Many Faces of a Liar 85

Chapter 6: The Body Rarely Lies 91

Chapter 7: Protecting Yourself from Character Assassination.. 97

Chapter 8: Stop Lying to Yourself................................ 104

8.1: You Do Have Time 108

8.2: Things Won't Get Any Better . . . Unless You Make Them Better... 111

Chapter 9: Ten Big Lies You Might Hear at Work 113

    1: There will be no bonuses or raises this year because 115

    2: Your salary is in line with what people of your experience and skill level are making. 115

    3: Let me talk that over with the powers that be. 115

    4: We've got a plan to turn things around. 116

    5: This is a temp-to-hire position. 116

    6: That's just a rumor 116

    7: We're all working toward the same goal............. 117

    8: The other person was more qualified................. 117

    9: We're implementing a hiring freeze................... 117

    10: We're looking for volunteers. 117

Chapter 10: What to Do When Your Kids Start Lying... 118

Chapter 11: Exposing Lies... 123

Preface

The intent of this book is to teach you about lies and how to tell when someone is lying. What you do with it is entirely up to you.

You can use it in your daily life to know when you're being deceived. It's tough to turn it off and on once you know what to look for, but you can try to use it selectively whenever it benefits you to know when someone is lying.

The information contained in this book is powerful stuff. You may think you want to know when you're being lied to, but once you realize how often you actually are being lied to, you may wish you could rewind time and unlearn the tips and techniques laid out in this book.

While estimates of how many lies a person is told a day varies widely, you could be told as many as a couple hundred lies a day depending on the line of work you're in and the people you associate with. Sometimes ignorance is bliss.

On the other hand, you may want to know when you're being lied to.

You may suspect you're being lied to and want to know the truth. In that case, you can use this book to your advantage. You can learn to tell when you're being lied to both in your personal life and at work. You can use your new knowledge to your advantage to further your career and to enhance your personal life. There's something to be said about cutting out all the dead weight in your life.

Sometimes the people you should be able to trust the most are the ones who are the least trustworthy.

In order to properly use the information in this book, you have to be able to distinguish between important lies and lies that are inconsequential. Trying to identify every last lie you're told and out the teller will leave you in a perpetual state of paranoia, not to mention the fact that you won't have any friends and your family won't want to be around you. Save the lie detection techniques for the important lies and let the little lies go.

There are only a select few people who know the lie detection tricks you're about to learn and even fewer who are able to lie without giving away the fact that they're lying.

After reading this book and putting what you've learned into practice, you'll be able to read other people like a book. A wide open book with big print. There will be those who are practiced liars who will be harder to read, but there are ways to tell they're lying, too. You won't be able to catch every single lie you're told, but you can drastically up your chances.

Chapter 1: Types of Lies

"There are three types of lies – lies, damn lies, and statistics."

- Benjamin Disraeli

In order to tell when people are lying, it's important to have an understanding of what lies are and why people tell them.

Lies are false statements made by a person with the intent to deceive. The person telling the lie knows he or she isn't telling the truth and is intentionally manipulating reality to fit their needs. A lie needn't be damaging to be classified as a lie, but it does have to be an intentional act of deception.

Three things must be present for an untruth to be considered a lie:

- **Incorrect information is being presented, either verbally or through omission.**
- **The information is known to be incorrect by the person presenting it.**
- **The intent behind presenting said information is to lead the recipient to believe it is true.**

Simply making a false statement doesn't automatically mean an individual is lying. At times, a person may make statements they don't realize are false. A false statement made under the pretense of truth isn't classified as a lie unless the person making the statement knows they're lying. If you tell someone that monkeys can fly and you truly believe it to be true because of something you've previously heard, you aren't lying; you're simply misinformed.

A person could spread inaccurate information that they actually believe to be true. They may have been lied to or had false information presented to them. They're guilty of not properly vetting the information they're passing along, but they aren't guilty of intentionally telling a lie.

This leads us to the second and third factors that must be present for deception to be classified as a lie. The person telling the lie must know the information they're presenting is not based in fact and they must be presenting it with the intent to mislead another person.

One might assume a person who is presenting something as fact when they know it isn't true would always be presenting this information with the intent to mislead. The reality is there are a small handful of cases in which one is exclusive of the other. Parody and sarcasm immediately come to mind. A person could present false information as a joke or as sarcasm under the pretense that the receiving party would understand that the information is false. If someone believes the information to be true, it isn't because the person who gave them the information is lying; it's because they misunderstood the context in which the information was presented.

Fiction is another grey area where misrepresentations are presented under the pretext of truth. An author creates fictional stories that everyone knows aren't true, but they read them and imagine they are. Is the author lying?

Absolutely not. He or she is creating a fictional word into which people willing dive into headfirst. They know the story isn't true, but like to be mislead into believing it is while they're reading it. Popular topics like science fiction and steampunk would be all but impossible to write without at least some stretching of the truth.

On the other hand, if an author writes a non-fiction book and fills it with lies and false stories that appear to prove his thesis correct, this is lying. People are buying the book believing the information inside to be true. Misleading them by knowingly presenting false information to prove your point is by definition a lie—and potentially a damaging one.

Just ask James Frey, who wrote a nonfiction memoir titled *A Million Little Pieces* that flew up the bestseller charts after it was recommended on the Oprah Winfrey show in 2005. Oprah nearly cried on camera when she spoke of the book, which Frey presented as his true account of his struggle with drugs and alcohol. After Winfrey recommended the book, it sat firmly entrenched in the number one spot on the New York Times bestseller nonfiction list for 17 weeks week straight.

The problem with this supposedly true retelling of Frey's life is that large chunks of the story were lies. Frey initially presented the book as entirely true, but later had to recant after *The Smoking Gun* revealed publicly that certain aspects of his story weren't true. It turned out large parts of his story were either embellishments of the truth or outright lies. Frey appeared on the Oprah Winfrey show and admitted to duping readers of the book.

When it came out that the book was full of lies, there was immediate outrage from fans of the book, as well as the people he'd told lies about in the book. Frey was sued multiple times and Frey and his publishing company eventually offered a refund of the cost of the book to every person who'd bought it up until a disclaimer was included in the book. Frey eventually moved with his family to France after he got tired of being in the public eye.

There's a popular misconception that all lies are told with malicious intent. This couldn't be further from the truth. Many lies are told to spare people from the truth. Can they still be damaging? Yes, but the intent isn't always to do harm. The fact that that a lie doesn't cause any harm doesn't make it any less of a lie—it just makes it a different type of lie.

The types of lies that are acceptable vary from culture to culture. They also vary from person to person within a culture. While one person may feel no guilt about telling a lie to further their career, everyone else be damned, another may be eaten up by guilt telling a small white lie that doesn't hurt a soul.

Most people will tell you lying is an evil act—that is, until they're the ones engaging in it. Then they'll tell you they're doing it for good reason. Lies never seem as bad or as damaging when you're the one telling them—and they always seem worse when you're the one being lied to.

People lie for a number of reasons. Here are the most common reasons people will lie:

- **Greed.** People will lie if they think they have something to gain by lying. Financial gains and the want of more power are two of the most prevailing reasons people lie.
- **Fear.** People lie because they're afraid of the repercussions of telling the truth. They want to avoid conflict and are worried people won't accept them for what they are.
- **Compassion.** This is something you wouldn't normally associate with lying, but there are lies told to spare people's feelings. A lie told because the truth is too hurtful is a lie of compassion.

There are a number of types of lies. Let's take a look at some of the more common lies people tell.

1.1: White Lies

White lies are lies told to avoid hurting the feelings of the person being lied to. They're generally harmless lies told because telling the lie is easier than telling the truth.

Very rare is the person who doesn't tell a white lie when the chance presents itself.

White lies are one of the few lies that are relatively harmless. When a wife asks her husband whether her butt looks big in a pair of jeans, and her butt looks humongous in said jeans, the husband is much better off telling a white lie. "No, sweetie. Your butt looks fine" is much easier than facing the wrath of an angry wife if he tells the truth.

These lies are more often than not told in the name of keeping the peace. Instead of causing problems, white lies are told to prevent even bigger problems from taking place. All but the most honest of people engage in the occasional white lie.

Here are some of the more common white lies you may encounter:

- You look fine; don't worry about it.
- Thank you! I love the gift.
- I'll be ready in a few minutes.
- I was just getting ready to call you.
- Thanks for dinner. It was delicious.
- I'll get right on that.
- I thought I did it already.
- That makes perfect sense.
- That's exactly what I would have done.

- I would have done things differently if I was there.
- I wouldn't have let that happen.
- Your baby is adorable.
- You're so smart. I admire what you do.
- I didn't realize you wanted it done that way.

While the lie detecting methods laid out in this book can be used to detect white lies, you're better off learning to let them go. Most people tell them, and calling someone out on a harmless white lie serves no purpose other than to create friction.

It helps to remember that white lies aren't told maliciously. The intent behind them is good.

No one likes being lied to, but learning to accept harmless white lies at face value will make your life easier and will go a long way toward keeping the peace. Save the confrontations for the bigger lies that actually matter.

1.2: Ethical Lies

To some, the title of this section may sound like an oxymoron. If lies are intentional deception, then how can one ethically lie?

One could make the argument that some white lies are ethical lies. If a lie is told so as not to hurt the other person's feelings, is it then an ethical lie? Take the ugly baby example. Is it ethical to tell a lie to someone about how attractive their baby is instead of telling them the truth about their ugly kid?

While purists will no doubt tell you no lie is a good lie, what then of a lie told to save the life of an innocent person?

A white man hiding an escaped slave in his home in colonial times might have lied to the people pursuing the slave in order to throw them off of his trail. The same sort of lies took place during the Holocaust when Germans allowed Jews to hide in their homes and lied to the Nazis when they were questioned. It would be tough to make an argument against this sort of lie being ethical. Sure, a lie is being told, but that lie is being told to save someone from a greater evil.

Here's another example. You see a woman running down the street. She's battered and bloody and ignores you when you ask her if she needs help. She reaches an intersection and turns left. Moments later an angry looking brute of a man pulls up in a car. He stops and rolls down the window and asks you gruffly if you've seen a woman run by. You notice there's blood on his hands. You ask the man what he wants the woman for and he tells you it's none of your business.

Taking the moral high ground of never telling a lie could result in the woman being badly hurt or even killed. You don't know what the man is up, but you can put two and two together. If you say yes, you've seen the woman and point him in the right direction, you could be signing the woman's death certificate.

You could lie and say you haven't seen the woman at all. This would give the woman a 50-50 chance of getting away. If the man reaches the end of the road and turns left, she's screwed. If he goes right, she's probably going to escape. As long as you're lying, would it be even more ethical to point the man in the wrong direction? Telling him she went right would almost assuredly buy her enough time for you to call the cops and tell them what you've just witnessed.

Ethical lies are lies told for the greater good.

The problem with this sort of lie is it's open to interpretation. What one person sees as an ethical reason to lie may not be ethical to another person. Where do you draw the line? Is it ethical to save a life? What about saving someone from physical harm? How about lying to save someone from losing their job?

It's tough to draw a line and make a distinction as to what is and isn't an ethical reason to lie. Concern for the wellbeing of others should trump obtuse honesty, but there's still a lot of grey area. What if a lie saves on person from harm, but puts another person in danger? What if a lie saves hundreds of people from harm, but takes the life of one person? While it may seem ethical from the point of view of the people being saved and their families, the sacrificial lamb may not feel the same way.

1.3: Lying By Omission

Lying by omission is lying by failing to correct something you know to be wrong or by omitting certain facts to skew a story in your favor. The words coming from your mouth aren't lies, but you're intentionally misleading someone by not telling them what you know to be the truth. If you allow someone to believe something you know to be inaccurate, you're lying by omission.

An example of lying by omission would be a man who dresses up as a doctor and goes door to door offering to give women a free breast exam. As long as he doesn't specifically tell them he's a doctor, he's guilty of lying by omission. In this case, it's a crime, as he's misrepresenting himself as a medical professional regardless of whether he actually tells them he's a doctor or not.

Children master lying by omission at an early age.

If you don't specifically ask a child something, chances are they aren't going to freely admit it if they think it's going to get them in trouble. A kid who allows his brother to take the fall for something he was in on is lying by omission. So is the brother who takes the fall if he doesn't tell his parents the other brother was involved, too.

Lying by omission is almost as bad as lying because it can completely change the way the person hearing something understands it.

Take the following short story for example:

Chris Carver (not a real person) got off early from work one afternoon and rushed home to surprise his girlfriend of seven years. When he got there, he found a strange vehicle in his driveway. He entered the house and heard his girlfriend screaming bloody murder from the bedroom. Chris rushed into the room and found a strange man attempting to have intercourse with his girlfriend. She was fighting to push him off of her and was yelling for him to stop. Chris picked up one of his softball bats from the corner of the room, walked over to the man and hit him once in the head, killing him instantly.

Now take the same short story with 2 sentences omitted:

Chris Carver (not a real person) got off early from work one afternoon and rushed home to surprise his girlfriend of seven years. When he got there, he found a strange vehicle in his driveway. Chris rushed into the room and found a strange man attempting to have intercourse with his girlfriend. Chris picked up one of his softball bats from the corner of the room, walked over to the man and hit him once in the head, killing him instantly.

In the original story, Chris sounds like a hero who saves his girlfriend from an attacker. The second story makes Chris appear to be a jilted lover who kills a man he finds his girlfriend in bed with. While neither story is telling outright lies, the second story leads you to believe something that isn't true. *It's a classic case of lying by omission.*

The media is often guilty of lying by omission. They only tell part of the story and skew it to suit their needs. Radio and television stations that lean toward one side of the fence or the other will often make huge stories of scandals they think will further their causes while largely ignoring the stories that aren't in line with their beliefs.

Politicians are also guilty of lying by omission. Have you ever heard the term *spin doctor*? A spin doctor is a person hired specifically to tell only part of the truth in order to get people's support.

In what may go down in history as the most famous lie by omission ever committed on a public stage, then President of the United States Bill Clinton publicly denied having sexual relations with Monica Lewinsky during his presidency. When evidence was later provided that showed he had received oral sex from her, he claimed he thought the definition of sexual relations included giving oral sex but not receiving it. Talk about omission!

Some people might argue that lying by omission isn't really lying because no lies are being told. Those who use this type of lie often justify it by saying they aren't really lying; they're just not giving up information they haven't been asked about.

Remaining silent when you know the truth is deceptive because it still manipulates the person being lied to into believing something that isn't true.

Masters of lying by omission are able to steer a conversation away from a topic they don't want to be forced into telling the truth about. Watch for this when you're wondering if someone is lying. If you bring something up and a person tries to change the topic without touching upon the subject matter, try pressing harder. There's probably something about that topic the person doesn't want you to know.

1.4: Bold-Faced Lie

The term *bold-faced* (or *barefaced* or *bald-faced*) lie is used to refer to a lie that's so obviously a lie everyone in the room knows it isn't true.

The terms barefaced or bald-faced liar more than likely stem from the fact that merchants and businessmen in the 18th century often wore large beards in order to hide the fact they were lying. A barefaced businessman was believed to have difficulty lying because it would be written all over his face.

The term bold-faced liar is relatively new and has only been in use for a short time. The context in which the term originated isn't known for sure and there are a couple theories as to where it came from. The first is that it's in reference to bold-faced type, which places emphasis on a word or passage. A bold-faced liar is bold enough to emphasize a lie when he knows the whole room is aware he isn't telling the truth.

The term bold-faced has also been attributed to the fact that a person telling such a lie has to be bold in order to tell it. The term bold-faced has been in use for quite some time and has only recently have lies been classified as bold-faced. This is more than likely the correct context in which the term bold-faced is used.

No matter what you call it, a bald-faced lie is one in which the fact that the person telling it is lying is common knowledge. The person telling the lie knows it isn't true and the audience knows it isn't true. This sort of lie is often told by people who are telling them in an effort to convince themselves the lie is true as much as they are trying to convince others.

A person who blindly supports an evil dictator will often tell everyone who listens what a good leader the dictator is. They refuse to listen to facts, instead choosing to disseminate false information in the hopes it'll one day become true.

Another example of a bold-faced lie is a criminal who's caught red-handed denying he committed a crime until his dying day. It's not uncommon for death row inmates to proclaim their innocence all the way up to the day of their execution, even in the face of overwhelming evidence to the contrary.

Bald-faced lies are often met with outrage, most likely because people can't believe the person telling them has the audacity to try to pass such a lie off as truth. The bald-faced liar knows his lie isn't going to be accepted as fact, but tells it anyway, truth be damned.

These are the easiest lies to detect because they are so far-fetched, so absurd, that it's painfully obvious they aren't true.

1.5: Fabrications

Fabrications are lies told with the intent of covering up or bending the truth. A fabrication is a made-up story that's designed to look like it's true. It may or may not be based in reality.

A teenage boy who makes up stories of his exploits with women to impress his friends is engaging in fabrication. He's telling stories that could be true and are believable, but never actually took place. Children will often fabricate entire stories of things that they say have taken place in their lives. Sometimes the stories they fabricate can be pretty far out there.

People often craft fabrications to further their careers and personal lives.

When it comes to work, resumes are full of fabrications and half-truths. Ask any hiring manager worth his salt how accurate the information found on résumés is and he'll tell you it's important to check references and make sure a candidate actually knows what he says he does. A company I once worked for interviewed and hired a man for a management position only to find out later that he couldn't read at more than a 3rd grade level. The man's résumé said he had a Bachelor's degree from an Ivy League college. It turned out he hadn't even graduated from junior high.

On the dating scene, fabrications are all too common. Just ask anyone who's responded to an online dating ad only to meet up with a completely different person than the one in the profile picture. The lies don't stop there. People will lie about the job they have, the things they enjoy, where they live and how much money they have in order to make themselves appear more interesting to a potential date.

Exaggeration and fabrication often walk hand-in-hand. Exaggerations take place when a person stretches the truth. If you were at the scene of a crime and did nothing, then went and told your friends you helped stop the crime, you are exaggerating about your involvement. Similarly, a teenage boy who kisses a girl after a date may go back and tell his friends he did more than that.

Fabrications can be one of the more damaging types of lies.

People make important decisions based on fabricated stories. These decisions can not only negatively impact the person being lied to; in some cases, they can endanger others. Imagine a doctor who lies about his credentials and is asked to treat a patient who has a rare disease. If the doctor has no clue what he is doing, the patient could die before he's found out.

1.6: Secondary Lies

A single lie often can't stand on its own. An old proverb states "*Lies have no legs,*" meaning lies are unable to stand on their own. For this reason, *secondary lies* often have to be told to support other lies that have been told.

Secondary lies are the reason most liars are caught. A person starts off by telling a lie. When questioned about the lie they've told, they have to tell secondary lies that support their story. Secondary lies then have to be told to support the secondary lies. Soon, an intricate web of lies has been created to support the original lie.

Eventually this web of deceit breaks down when the person doing the lying reaches a point where they've told so many lies they can't keep up with them.

Most liars aren't caught lying because of the original lie they told. They're caught once their web of secondary lies begins to unravel. This is the reason police interrogate suspects for hours. They ask question after question until the web of lies is so tangled and convoluted it's impossible to keep track of. The seemingly unimportant question they ask early in the investigation may be something they come back to later to see if a person remembers it. A person telling the truth won't have a problem recalling minor details. A person who's lying, on the other hand, may not remember a minor detail they lied about hours after the fact.

Lies that keep growing and growing to the point they're out of control are called *chronic lies*. A person engaged in chronic lying often leads a life built on lies. They lie so often they even have trouble distinguishing their lies from reality.

1.7: Denial

***Denial* is another common form of lying. When a person lies by denial, they refuse to acknowledge something they know is a truth.**

People usually engage in denial to keep themselves out of trouble. A student caught cheating on a test may deny that he was cheating in an effort to stay out of trouble. If the student admits to cheating, he may be suspended or expelled. If he continues denying he cheated, there's a chance he may convince others of his innocence.

There are people who will passionately deny something even when they're caught red-handed. Criminals caught in the act will often plead their innocence in front of a judge and jury in the hopes they can convince them they didn't commit the crimes they're accused of. As long as they're denying it, there's a chance they could go free. Once they make an admission of guilt, they're headed to the big house, albeit sometimes with a lesser sentence.

Denial is often a form of self-preservation. It's also used to avoid having to make whole-scale changes in one's life.

People who engage in denial do so because they either don't want to face the truth themselves, or they don't want others to know the truth about them. Drug addicts and alcoholics will deny they have a problem when confronted with their addictions. It often takes hitting rock bottom before an addict or alcoholic is willing to face the truth.

Denial shows its face in many forms:

- **Blaming someone else; often the victim.**
- **Unreasonable justification of one's actions.**
- **Minimizing the truth in order to make it appear less harmful than it actually is.**
- **Avoiding taking responsibility for one's actions.**
- **Lying about a fact.**
- **Denying the consequences of one's actions.**
- **Denial of the severity of one's actions.**

Denial is such a powerful force people will even deny that they're in denial. This allows them to continue down the current path they're on without having to make any changes in their lives. People in denial often aren't just lying to others; they're lying to themselves as well.

1.8: Minimization

People who make a costly mistake will often attempt to *minimize* it in the eyes of others. They'll play it down in an attempt to make it look less costly than it actually is.

Minimization seeks to work on two levels. It attempts to minimize mistakes in the eyes of others and it helps the person who made the mistake rationalize it. If they're able to convince themselves and others that a mistake isn't that big of a deal, they won't have to worry about it anymore.

Reduction words are words people use to minimize something. The following phrases and words are common denominators you can look for if you suspect minimization is taking place:

- All I did was . . .
- I just . . .
- Sort of . . .
- It wasn't really . . .
- Only a little . . .
- It's not that big of . . .
- Kind of . . .
- Merely . . .
- Simply . . .
- Barely . . .
- Hardly . . .
- I didn't know/mean to/realize . . .
- I'm sorry . . .

Also look for attempts to divorce results from the action that brought them forth. A person who says "I just threw the rock over the fence; I didn't realize a person was there" when confronted by someone who got hit by a rock is looking to remove the action from the consequence.

Minimization is a common form of deception in cases where feeling are hurt or charges are filed over spoken words. "I was just joking. I didn't mean anything by it" is an attempt to minimize a statement made, regardless of the initial intent.

Chapter 2: Types of Liars

"Actually," said Jace, "I prefer to think that I'm a liar in a way that's uniquely my own."

— Cassandra Clare, *City of Ashes*

Liars are said to be two-faced because they show one face to the person they're lying to while the reality is they have another completely different face they're keeping out of sight. It's similar to a person wearing a mask in that you don't see the real person; you only see a façade the person has put up to fool you.

There are as many types of liar as there are types of lies. In order to fully understand a person and to figure out whether or not they're lying, it helps to know what type of liar they are.

Before we get into the types of liar, I want you to be aware that people rarely fit into just one of these categories. It isn't uncommon for a person to be completely honest with the people he or she cares about and to be more than willing to lie to the people who don't matter to them. You might also find a person who is honest at work, but lies to his or her friends and family. Some people are all over the place when it comes to lies. Some days they might lie constantly, while other days they go the whole day without lying. In some areas of their life they may lie about everything, while they're generally honest in other areas.

Let's take a look at the various types of liar you may encounter.

2.1: The Pathological Liar

The scientific term for a pathological liar is *pseudologica fantastica*. It is defined as extensive falsification for no discernible reason. The pathological liar lies just to lie, with no real reason or intent behind their lies.

Amy Tucker dated a pathological liar. She says it was like dating a chameleon. One moment he was telling her he'd worked for 3 years on a NASCAR pit crew; the next he was claiming he'd been part of the group that staged the NASA moon landing. Over the 2 years she was with him, her boyfriend told her so many lies it was impossible to keep up with all of them.

"It was as if he lived in a fantasy world; one he created to make his life appear as though it was the most interesting life ever lived. Jackson told me he'd been commissioned by the President to hunt down Fidel Castro and narrowly missed a chance to assassinate him in the early 80's. He had an entire story he'd fabricated about how he had him in his sights, but had to back off because he was worried about hitting the wrong person in the crowd. The first time he told the story he was a Navy Seal, and then it changed to an Army Ranger later on down the road. I was impressed with his stories at first, but they all turned out to be bull," Amy said when asked about living with a pathological liar.

Pathological liars live in a world based more on fantasy than on reality.

They tell stories that could be true and may have a sliver of truth somewhere inside them, but the truth has been stretched so far it's no longer in the same ballpark as what it originally was. A pathological liar who met a celebrity and shook his hand might tell people the celebrity invited him to his house for drinks and they partied the night away. He'd concoct an entire story around the chance meeting, weaving a tapestry of lies to make the meeting and handshake much larger than it was. There's a sliver of truth in the story, as the man did meet the celebrity, but the rest of the story is a made-up fantasy.

Pathological liars are often believed to be delusional because they're able to create intricate and detailed stories of their exploits. A pathological liar isn't always delusional because the person telling the lies more often than not knows they're telling a lie. They'll try to make you believe it, but may backtrack and admit they're lying if presented with hard evidence that disproves what they've been telling people. A delusional individual believes the lies they're telling are true and will insist they aren't lying even when presented with overwhelming evidence to the contrary.

There are cases in which pathological liars are so delusional that they don't know they're lying.

When this occurs, it's called *false memory syndrome*. The sufferer has lied so much about an event or so badly wants it to be true they create a fake memory of the event. The false memories are usually grandiose in nature and paint the sufferer in either a particularly good or bad light.

An acquaintance of mine works with a pathological liar who has three missing front teeth. The man tells anyone who will listen the story of how he was one of the workers who helped build the Superdome stadium that the New Orleans Saints play in and was working one day on the peak of the dome and fell off. He claims he landed face-first and walked away from the fall with just the three missing teeth.

There are a number of inconsistencies with this story. One, a fall from the top of Superdome would mean the man fell more than 250 feet. No one walks away from a fall like that. Had he of survived that sort of fall, it would have been a miracle. Surviving a fall like that with only a couple teeth being knocked out would have made him a living legend. The second, and perhaps most telling, piece of evidence that this story is a lie is that the man is 45 years old. That would mean he was working at the top of the Superdome when he was somewhere in the range of 5 to 10 years old.

My friend got tired of hearing this story and one day started questioning it. When he asked the man whether there were any witnesses, he was told the whole crew had seen it. My friend pointed out that it would have made the man a living legend if anyone witnessed it. The man told him he'd asked the crew not to say anything because he didn't want all the attention. After a few more questions and a few more lies, my friend hit him with the whopper. When he asked the man if he realized that he couldn't have been more than 10 years old when the Superdome was completed in the early 70's the man immediately told him he'd been big for his age and had a mustache and had fooled the foreman into thinking he was 18.

Lying is a character trait for the pathological liar. They lie in response to almost everything and show little to no remorse about lying. They engage in lies so often, it becomes a way of life and is second nature.

When presented with an opportunity to lie, a pathological liar almost always lies so that they will be seen in a more favorable light. While this may work in the short-term, the long-term implications can have dire consequences. Pathological liars often end up alone because they've alienated themselves from their friends and family members because of their lies. Even if they do have family and friends willing to put up with them, they're often the laughingstock of the family of circle of friends because of their propensity for lying.

The urge to lie in a pathological liar is so strong that it's classified as a mental illness. The symptoms and extent of the disease hasn't been extensively studied and as of now there's no one-size-fits-all cure.

2.2: The Opportunistic Liar

The opportunistic liar doesn't lie for no reason, but has no compunction about lying when it suits his needs. This sort of liar may lie frequently or only on occasion, depending on how often they feel lying will help them get ahead in life.

Opportunistic lies are guided by selfish motives and are told when the opportunistic liar thinks they will benefit them.

It's tough to identify opportunistic lies by taking them at face value because they're usually well thought out and are told with a strategic purpose in mind. Politicians engage in opportunistic lying while on the campaign trail. They make all sorts of promises they fail to live up to once elected. They get in trouble if they spread false rumors about other candidates, but they've been known to push their cohorts to spread rumors that aren't true.

The bigger the potential gain, the more likely an opportunistic liar is to make up a lie to fit the situation. Opportunistic liars are often seen as go-getters because they have everyone fooled into thinking their lies are the truth. Salesmen and businessmen often engage in opportunistic lying. A car salesman who tells a potential buyer there's nothing wrong with a car when he knows the brakes are going to have to be replaced is engaging in opportunistic lying.

Opportunistic lies can also be used to make one candidate for a position look like a better choice than the other candidates. A person who's trying to get promoted may make up stories about another person they're competing with for a job and spread them around work with the hope they'll get back to the boss. They may also make up stories about themselves so they'll appear better than they actually are.

Opportunistic lies are rarely victimless lies. The person telling the lie usually seeks to gain something at the expense of someone else.

2.3: The Unskilled Liar

The unskilled liar doesn't lie very often and isn't very good at lying. They will lie from time to time, but the lies they tell are rarely harmful. In the event a lie they tell does do harm, they find themselves racked with guilt.

It's easy to tell when an unskilled liar isn't telling truth because it's written all over their face. They won't make eye contact with you, will be shifting from side to side and everything about their demeanor and actions will scream out guilty.

While a skilled liar is able to tell a lie without batting an eye, the unskilled liar is acutely aware when they are lying and is scared to death of getting caught. They'll often break down and admit to a lie if they suspect they're in danger of getting caught. A confrontation will almost always result in an admission of guilt and an apology.

There are a number of people who are honest almost all the time because they aren't skilled at lying or don't like the way it makes them feel. These people are respected by their peers and are trusted by friends and family alike. They may still tell a lie once in a while to spare someone's feelings or to further a good cause, but they don't engage in destructive lying that might harm others.

Most people are unskilled liars on a subconscious level. They don't like to lie and try not to tell lies unless they have to.

Some people are worse than others when it comes to exposing themselves through their words and actions, but it's rare to find a person who is so good at lying they can't be read. Interestingly enough, many people who think they're good at lying are actually giving themselves away in a number of ways.

2.4: The Smooth Operator

You're going to have a tough time telling when a smooth operator is lying. They're skilled liars who have made lying their craft, and they work and manipulate the spoken word to suit their needs.

Not only do smooth operators engage in flat-out lies, they also bend the truth and spin what they're saying to get you to think one thing while they're saying another. If you call them out on something you think is inaccurate, they'll talk their way out of it and leave you looking like you're clueless as to what the fact of the matter is.

Even the experts in lie detection have a tough time picking out the lies a smooth operator is telling.

It can be done, but it's going to take paying close attention to detail because the normal keys and cues won't be present. Smooth operators may be studied in the mannerisms and speech patterns used by liars and have practiced lying enough to avoid them, or they may instinctively be able to avoid giving themselves away. Either way, it's tough to tell when they're lying.

It can be fun to watch a smooth operator at work when you know he's spinning a tall tale. They've got lying down to an art form. Even when you know a person is a smooth operator and is capable of lying, it's tough not to fall for their lies.

Smooth operators are usually intelligent, witty people who are charismatic and popular. They hang out with people who hang on their every word and eat up their lies hook, line and sinker.

2.5: The Sociopathic Liar

Sociopathic liars are similar to pathological liars in that they live a life filled with lies. They feel driven to lie and feel no guilt when they do regardless of the impact of their lies on those around them.

A sociopath almost never tells the truth. Everything that comes out of their mouth is a lie.

They tell a lie, and then they spend countless hours considering the lie from all angles so they're able to tell even more lies to support the original lie. They lie to cover up mistakes, to get ahead in life and to make themselves look and feel better than the people around them. They also lie just to lie.

When sociopathic liars are caught in a lie, they'll tell even more lies and will continue lying no matter what. It doesn't matter what evidence you present or whether or not there were witnesses; the sociopathic liar will continue lying. They believe that as long as they don't admit they are guilty, there's going to be a sliver of doubt in the minds of the people they're lying to. They'll keep working at that sliver until they've got everyone so confused they don't know what's going on.

There's no blaming a sociopathic liar for something. It's always someone else's fault and there's always a good (at least in their eyes) reason why things happened the way they did. They look at life differently than the normal person does. The world is a largely emotionless place to the sociopath. They don't feel guilt, so it's nothing for them to push their problems off on an innocent person. Their main concern in a crisis situation is personal damage control, everyone else be damned.

Sociopathic liars are so robotic and so adept at lying they are able to pass lie detector tests. They don't show or feel emotion, so the normal things a lie detector test shows when a person lies doesn't show up when a sociopathic liar tells a lie.

You are going to have a tough time catching a sociopathic liar in a lie because they refuse to be caught.

You might convince others that the person is lying, but you'll never get an admission of guilt from them—that is, unless they feel they have something to gain by admitting guilt. They may be more than willing to admit guilt to something small if they feel it will allow them to pawn off getting in trouble for something even bigger.

2.6: The Polite Liar

Some people are polite to a fault, as is the case with the polite liar. This type of liar doesn't tell lies for personal gain, they tell lies in a misguided attempt to help others or spare other people's feelings. You know the type. There's always one person in the office who's overly polite and agrees with everything.

The polite liar is so worried about being nice and making sure everyone is happy with them that they are incapable of taking a stand and telling people how they feel.

Ask them if they're busy or if they have time to help you and they'll tell you they have time to help even when they're swamped. Ask them if it's OK for you to do something and they'll tell you it is even if they disagree with what you're doing. Ask them their opinion on something and they'll tell you what they think you want to hear.

The biggest fault of the polite liar is their inability to tell people that they disagree with something. They'll lie and lie about something until it reaches a boiling point. Once they reach a certain point, the polite liar goes from nice guy to hothead in no time flat and acts like you're supposed to be able to read their mind.

Polite liars rarely hurt anyone other than themselves with their lies, but they tend to burn out quickly since they spend their lives trying to please others with little regard paid to their own personal needs.

Chapter 3: How to Protect Yourself from Lies

"The truly scary thing about undiscovered lies is that they have a greater capacity to diminish us than exposed ones. They erode our strength, our self-esteem, our very foundation."

— Cheryl Hughes

In a perfect world, we'd be able to blindly trust everyone we came in contact with, knowing they weren't capable of lying to us. This isn't a perfect world, so it's imperative that we preemptively seek to minimize the damage caused by lies.

The best way to protect yourself from lies is to constantly be on the lookout for situations in which lies are likely to be told, and then to assess whether or not a lie being told is damaging enough for you worry about. If it's a victimless lie, you're probably better off just letting it go. On the other hand, if the lie is potentially damaging to you or others, you may want to take a closer look at it.

Sometimes you're better off letting a lie pass unchecked.

Other than close friends and family (and sometimes not even them), there aren't very many people in the world you can trust. The problem with trusting nobody is you eventually find yourself constantly searching for lies while wandering the world alone and in a perpetual state of paranoia. That's no way to live, so you're better off picking and choosing the situations where you want to watch closely.

Some situations just don't warrant close examination.

If you're at the nail salon getting a pedicure and the nail lady is telling you a fantastic story, it's best to accept it at face value and not worry about whether parts of the story are fabricated. On the other hand, if you're at the salon and the nail lady tells you your cuticles are badly damaged and you need an expensive new treatment, it's time to turn on your spider sense and watch for signs that she's being less than truthful.

Anytime you're being pressured to make a purchase—and especially a big one—you're going to want to be on high alert. Appliances, vehicles, real estate, insurance. You name it, if there's a lot of money to be made, there are people out there willing to lie to get you to buy it. The bigger the potential payout, the bigger the lies.

Another place where lying is commonplace is at work. You find there are people willing to tell lies to get ahead no matter how much damage it causes other people. If you hear someone lying and it directly affects you, your best bet is usually to calmly confront the person telling the lies with the truth. They'll often recant what they've said and will be wary of telling lies that involve you in the future because they know you'll call them on it.

The most damaging lies aren't the ones you hear in person.

The lies told behind your back are going to cause you the most problems because they can change people's opinion of you without you ever finding out about it. The best way to preemptively strike against this sort of lie is to always be honest and act with the utmost integrity. If people see what a good person you are, they're less likely to believe it if someone says something bad about you behind your back.

3.1: The Truth Bias

Imagine a world where every single person walked around suspecting every statement they were told was a lie. Everyone would be under suspicion and no one could be trusted. It would be a world filled with distrust and deceit. The world would become an angry, bitter place.

Humans, by nature, are a trusting bunch. As children, we're taught that honesty is best policy and it eventually becomes a core belief. We like to believe the world is a good place with only a few bad seeds, so we're (for the most part) willing to blindly trust the people we encounter. We're often shocked when we become victims of our core beliefs because we like to believe everyone else on the planet is just like us.

We aren't honest 100% of the time, but most of us try to live as honest of a life as possible. We hope that those around us will do the same thing. For the most part, we're willing to believe people are who they say they are. Society has a system of checks and balances in place that gives us comfort where it's necessary, but for the most part we take what people tell us at face value.

We don't ask a butcher for his credentials to cut meat or for a veterinarian to show us her diploma when we take our beloved pets in for work. Even when we suspect that we're being lied to, we're willing to shrug it off as unimportant if it doesn't impact us directly.

This propensity for humans to blindly trust others even though we know there are dishonest people out there is called the *truth bias*.

When there's a situation in which we can give someone the benefit of the doubt without putting our life and limb at risk, we usually default to trust. The truth bias is so ingrained into human nature that most of the time we don't even realize we're blindly trusting people. When you go to a restaurant, do you ask to take a look at the kitchen before you sit down to eat? No, because you trust that the kitchen is going to be clean and sanitary. Do you ask the policeman who pulls you over to provide proof that he's an officer of the law? No, you trust that the flashing lights, the police car and the uniform all mean the person pulling you over is indeed and officer of the law. Do you run a background check on all of your children's teachers? No, again the truth bias is at play.

There are those amongst us who are more careful than others, but even they have to have at least a rudimentary level of trust in their fellow man. A person who attempted to check on every single thing they were told, while investigating every new place they entered and verifying the identity of everyone they met would never get anything done. Those who prefer to err on the side of caution may be careful in some areas, but they have to show at least some level of trust to get by in life.

Without truth bias, society would come to a screeching halt.

People are willing to accept a certain level of deception when it doesn't harm them or when the potential consequences aren't steep. Some people have more of a truth bias than others. People with a high level of bias are said to be *gullible*, because they believe anything they're told. Con men and scam artists make careers of seeking out these people and taking advantage of them. They're also constantly on the lookout for ways to sucker people with a lesser truth bias in.

Would it surprise you to find out you're being lied to in 26.2 percent of your daily communications? In a research study done by Cornell University titled *Deception and Design: The Impact of Communication on Lying Behavior*, 30 students tracked their social communications for 7 days. The students participated in an average of 6.11 communications per day and lied 1.6 times on average per day. This averages out to 26.2 percent of conversations during the day involving a lie. Sure, most of the lies being told aren't all that important, but we're being lied to a lot more than we think.

In order to avoid being deceived, you have to lower your truth bias. There's no need to wear a tin foil hat and watch for conspiracy everywhere you go. That would make for a miserable life. All I'm suggesting is you question the things that need to be questioned. Don't blindly trust people when you have a lot to lose.

Lower your truth bias and heighten your awareness and you'll be a lot less likely to be victimized.

3.2: Honing Your Deception Detection Skills

If you're the type of person who's gullible enough to believe anything and everything you're told, you're going to need to hone your deception detection skills.

Deception detection is the first step in identifying and outing a lie.

Gullible people are easily taken advantage of because they don't look at life with a skeptical eye. They're optimists that look at the world through rosy-tinted glasses and see the glass as half-full instead of half-empty. This allows liars to quickly identify and take advantage of them. Liars and con-men seek this sort of person out and milk them for everything they've got.

Take the story of Matt Johnson and his mother for example.

Matt worked a factory job for barely more than minimum wage. He lived with his mother and sister in a one-bedroom apartment. The three of them were barely making ends meet. Regardless of their struggles, Matt and his family were happy people and were thankful for what they had. They always had food on the table and they had a roof over their heads, which is more than what a lot of people have.

Matt believed in karma and knew one day he was going to catch a break. He was a good person and good people are eventually rewarded for their efforts at being good.

One Friday morning, Matt's mother woke him up early to tell him she had great news. She'd just received a phone call from a man in Jamaica telling her she'd won the Jamaican lottery. The caller told her she'd won a couple hundred thousand dollars and a car. When the mother told him she hadn't entered the lottery, the man said it wasn't uncommon for friends and family members to enter a ticket or two in someone else's name for good luck.

There is one catch, the man said. The Jamaican Embassy requires that all taxes on winnings are paid up front. Once the taxes are paid, the check would be delivered and the car would be shipped to her address immediately. The "good news" is the taxes in Jamaica aren't excessively high. The woman only had to pay $1,875.87 in taxes to claim her winnings.

Matt and his mother were ecstatic.

Matt called his boss to quit his job, explaining to him that he'd just won the Jamaican lottery. Sensing something was awry, Matt's boss told him that he was about to become a victim of fraud and should look into things a little closer before sending the money. When Matt insisted this was legitimate, his boss told him to be careful and let Matt know his job would be available if he needed it back.

The "lottery official" that had called Matt's mother asked that they send the money that day via Western Union. Matt and his family scrounged up every last penny they had and just had enough to pay the taxes on their winnings. They went to Western Union and were all set to send the money to Jamaica. Luckily, the person working behind the counter recognized the scam and let them know they were being defrauded. Disappointed, they went home and nursed their bruised egos. Matt sheepishly returned to work the next day and endured a good bit of teasing from his boss and co-workers.

Matt and his family got lucky. A lot of people don't. It's estimated that *billions* of dollars are lost to fraud every year. That's billions with a b.

While some of the money lost to fraud is lost due to circumstances that are out of the control of the person losing the money, a good chunk of it is lost by people like Matt and his mother. People who for one reason or another aren't good at detecting lies. In fact, it's estimated that $80 million a year is lost to the Jamaican lottery scam alone.

That's a heck of a lot of people falling for something they should know isn't legitimate.

There are a bunch of warning signs Matt, his sister and his mother chose to ignore. The fact that they hadn't entered the lottery should have been a big one. Another sign was the fact that the lottery they were told they'd won was in Jamaica. The prize being a couple hundred thousand dollars *and a car* seems a bit strange. Most lotteries just give away money. The taxes needing to be sent in upfront and the small amount should have been the biggest warning sign of them all. The fact that Matt's boss told him he was about to lose his money should have made Matt pause and think things through, but even that wasn't enough to keep him from heading to Western Union.

The only reason Matt and his family didn't lose their life savings was pure luck. The scam is a well-known scam and Western Union employees know about it. That was the only thing that stopped them from losing everything.

Being skilled at deception detection would have helped Matt and his mother identify the scam long before they headed over to Western Union. By looking at the situation with a skeptical eye, they would have seen a lot of warning signs that something wasn't right. In this day and age, information is only a click of the mouse or two away and they could have searched Google for "Jamaican lottery scam" and found out they were about to get ripped off. Even if they just searched "Jamaican lottery," they would have found a number of sites indicating the lottery they thought they'd won was a scam.

Con artists and scammers rely on the fact that there are a number of people out there who are gullible by nature.

Some people have such a low level of deception detection that even the most obvious of lies don't set off alarms in their heads. Most people would have instantly known the Jamaican lottery call was a scam and hung up. The scammers know it's a numbers game and make call after call until they find someone willing to believe their lies. 30,000 people a year report falling for it and it's estimated that only 10% of the people who fall for it actually report it. That means there are somewhere in the neighborhood of 300,000 people falling for just this scam every year. And there are thousands of similar scams out there.

Another common scam is a mass e-mail sent from someone claiming to be the patriarch of a wealthy Nigerian family. It's a cry for help asking that you pay the "small" legal fees required to help them get a large sum of money out of their country. In return, they offer to give you a cut of the money. It's estimated that hundreds of millions of dollars have been lost to this scam. It's been around in one form or the other since the 1920's.

How do you protect yourself from both scammers and liars alike? It's simple. With a little bit of common sense, you can employ deception detection techniques to identify when you're being lied to.

Whenever you're in a situation where you suspect you're being lied to, ask yourself the following questions:

1: Does this sound too good to be true?

There are situations in life where good things happen to good people. People win the lottery. People get great deals on expensive items. People find and fall in love with the perfect person for them. That said, most of the time life is imperfect. *Situations that seem too good to be true usually are.*

If a situation seems too good to be true, it doesn't have to automatically be classified as a lie. That would prevent you from taking advantage of situations that actually are as good as they seem. However, noting that a situation seems too good to be true should set off a warning alarm in your head.

Take a close look at anything that seems too good to be true. You may find out you've stumbled upon something great, but you may also save yourself a lot of heartburn and heartache over the long run.

2: What do I know of the person making the statement?

If you know the person and know they're generally truthful, chances are you're being told the truth. There's an outside chance the person is giving you incorrect information that they themselves believe to be true, so don't use this as your only determining factor.

On the other hand, if you don't know the person at all, you need to closely examine everything you're told, especially if the person has something to gain by lying. Salesmen are especially tricky in this regard. They've been known to tell whatever lies they have to in order to get people to make a purchase. Not all salesmen are dishonest. Most of them are good people, but there are enough bad seeds out there to warrant you taking everything you're told with a grain of salt.

You may find yourself in a conversation with a person you know to be dishonest. Your best bet in this situation is to assume everything you're being told is a lie. If something piques your interest, you can investigate it further, but always assume it's untrue until proven otherwise. This will protect you from being suckered into believing something that isn't true.

3: Are there parts of what you're being told that don't ring true?

Use common sense. If parts of a story sound fabricated or don't make sense, chances are you're being lied to. When something doesn't feel right, you need to be on high alert.

There may be parts of what you're being told that you know for a fact aren't true. When you come across a situation in which you know at least some of the information being presented is inaccurate, assume all of the information being presented is inaccurate. Don't commit to anything until you've had a chance to verify the rest of the information.

Arming yourself with as much knowledge as possible will help you identify when you're being lied to. Liars are able to lie because the people they're lying to don't have enough information to tell that they're lying. By gathering that information beforehand, you're going to put yourself in a position to detect deception while it's happening instead of after you've already been made a fool.

Want to see a liar squirm? Go to a meeting with a liar with more knowledge of the topic he's lying about than he has, and then point out all of the inaccuracies in his stories. I don't recommend doing this to your boss, but it can be fun at presentations or sales meetings where you have nothing to lose.

4: What does this person have to gain by lying?

While some people lie just to lie, most liars don't start fabricating stories unless they have something to gain from them. The bigger the gain, the bigger the chance the person is lying.

Try to look at things from the point of view of the other person. If someone tells you they're selling the best product on the market, what they're really telling you is they're not sure their product can stand on its own two feet. Ask them to prove to you that it's the best by comparing the features of their product with the other competing products on the market.

The same thing goes for your personal life. If you're on an online dating site and have met a person who seems like the perfect mate for you, don't let yourself fall for them until you've seen that what they're telling you is true. That perfect man or woman with their own house, a nice car and a great job may turn out to be a bum living in their mother's basement. Not that living in your mother's basement is a problem . . . It's only a problem if you lie about it in order to attract someone under a false pretext.

5: Is there a way for me to verify whether the statement is true or false?

Liars have it tough nowadays. Most people carry a lie detector with them everywhere they go. You do have a lie detector with you, don't you? OK, maybe you don't know it as a lie detector. Most people call it a cell phone.

Before you go searching the App Store for the latest and greatest lie detection app, let me tell you that lie detection isn't done via an application or a piece of software. It's done via the Internet. As long as you have an Internet connection, you have a world of information at your fingertips that can be used to verify statements of fact.

You can act like you're checking a text message and instead discreetly verify the information you're being given when you suspect you're being told a lie. Or you can simply tell the person that you want to verify the information you're being given and watch them squirm as you look it up in front of them. A person who's being honest won't be bothered by this at all. A person who's lying will act like it's a personal affront that you would dare think they're lying to you.

If you have a smart phone, you can do your research beforehand and create a document packed full of key information you want to remember. Keep it handy and reference it whenever you want to check on a fact.

Searching the Internet for information won't allow you to detect every lie, but it will allow you to verify most facts on the spot.

In the event you can't verify the truth of a statement by looking it up online, there may be other means through which it can be verified. You can discreetly ask around or you can go straight to the source. If you suspect a lie is being told about another person, that person will probably appreciate it if you go straight to them and ask them about what you heard. If it's a lie, they'll be glad to be able to set the story straight. If it's the truth, well, that can get a little sticky, but you can tactfully back of out the conversation. At least you'll know it's the truth. Be aware that the person you're asking to verify a story might lie about it if it's damaging enough.

Where there's a will, there's a way and most statements can be verified in one way or another. It's up to you to decide whether the ends justify the means. If verifying a story you've been told requires going to a person's friends and family and interviewing them to get the facts, it's up to you to decide whether it's worth it or not. You may be better off leaving well enough alone and just accepting you might never know the truth.

6: If I were listening to this person make this statement to someone else, would I believe it to be true?

Sometimes it helps to remove oneself from a situation and to look at it from someone else's point of view. Your ability to judge something that is relevant to you can be clouded by your desire to believe or disbelieve what you're being told. When you want something to be true you're more likely to believe it to be so. If you don't want something to be true, you're less likely to believe it to be true, regardless of the facts you've been presented.

Detaching yourself from a situation can be difficult. It helps to have a close friend or someone you know you can trust to run stuff by. When you suspect you're being lied to, tell them the facts and get their opinion on it. It may turn out that they can provide valuable insight or are able to point out an inconsistency you missed because your judgment is clouded.

7: What is the cost to me (or others I care about) if this is a lie?

Sometimes it's best to let a lie be a lie. White lies and lies that aren't particularly damaging to anything other than the credibility of the person telling them are better off left alone. That is, unless you want to discredit the person telling them to prove a point.

Victimless lies are lies that don't harm anyone and there's little to no harm done by them. These lies are better off left alone. You'll do more harm by pursuing them than would be done if you shrug them off.

3.3: Watch What They Say

When you suspect you're being lied to, you're going to want to pay attention to the words the suspected liar is using in his speech. There are certain words that are commonly used by people when they tell a lie. The presence of these words doesn't automatically mean a person is lying, but frequent use of them may indicate something isn't right.

Listen for the following words when you're wondering if you're being lied to:

Use of the word "that" when describing people or things may indicate a person is feeling guilty about the item or person they're talking about. For example, a woman who's been accused of cheating may refer to the person she's been cheating with as "that man" instead of "him" when confronted. "I didn't have sex with *that man*" isn't an admission of guilt, but there's good reason to be suspicious and to probe into it further.

Look for softening of harsh words. A guilty murderer who's directly asked if he killed a woman may respond with "I didn't *hurt* anyone" instead of using the word kill. This is an attempt to soften the guilt associated with what was done.

Words that allow the person telling the lie to stall and think of an answer almost always indicate dishonesty. When you ask a person a direct question and they respond with something to the effect of "Why would you even ask me a question like that? Don't you trust me?" they're stalling for time. They haven't thought up an answer to the question you've just asked them and are trying to buy some time so they can think it through.

Another stalling tactic is to repeat the question back to you or to ask you to repeat it. If you ask a person if they've been working on a report and they haven't started it yet, they might respond to your question with something along the lines of "The report that's due tomorrow? Let's see, have I started the report that's due tomorrow . . ." or "Report? Which report are you talking about?" They know exactly what report you're talking about. They're repeating the question to try to buy enough time to think up a suitable answer.

Use of overly polite words like "sir," "ma'am" or "boss" from a person who normally doesn't use them is another indicator a person is feeling guilty about something. They're deferring power to you by being polite and hoping it makes them appear weak and incapable of lying.

Use of the word "but" is indicative of a lie. "I know you're not going to believe this, *but* . . ." is usually followed by a lie.

Be on the lookout for the person being questioned to use a guarded tone when asked a question. If the person goes completely silent, then whispers "Are you accusing me of doing something wrong here?" they've got something to hide.

Watch for words that are stronger than what the situation calls for. If you ask someone if they sexually harassed another person at work and they simply say "No, I didn't do it," they might be telling the truth. If, on the other hand, they jump back and say "Absolutely not, I would never, ever think of doing such a thing," there's a good chance they're feeling guilty about what they've done and are overreacting to your question because of the guilt they feel.

Listen for phrases that attempt to convince you something is true. The phrases "To be completely honest with you" and "The truth is" are usually followed by a lie or a half-truth. Honest people don't need to add qualifiers to truthful statements. Liars add them to make themselves appear more honest.

Watch for unnecessary additions to answers. A person who tells you what a good and honest person they are after telling you they didn't steal office supplies afterhours is feeling guilty about something.

Liars rarely use contractions when they're telling lies. "I *didn't* do it" is more likely to be true than "I *did not* do it."

Watch for the "exit-route" statements. A person telling lies may attempt to leave themselves an exit route in case they're caught in their lies. Phrases like "I think what happened was . . ." and "My memory on the topic is a little hazy, but . . ." leave the liar a way to cop out if they think they're going to get caught.

Look for meaningless words to break up any pauses. "Uh," "ummm" and "like" are all meaningless words that are added to sentences when a person needs a bit more time to think up an answer. Long periods of silence also indicate a person is carefully choosing their words.

The key to successfully watching what a person says for items that may indicate deception is underway is to pay attention to them when you know they aren't lying and watch for *baseline behavior*. Once you have a baseline of how a person normally acts, you can use that baseline to watch for deviations from the norm. An example of this would be a person who normally uses contractions in his speech all of suddenly stopping use of them when talking about something you suspect they may be lying about.

Pay close attention to any pauses or breaks in a person's speech. If a person pauses on what you believe to be a minor detail, don't fill in the blanks for them. Listen to what's said and let the person you suspect is lying explain things in their own words.

When you're questioning someone for the first time, ask them open-ended questions that require more than a yes or no answer. Listen to their speech patterns and watch for verbal cues that they're lying. Open-ended questions require more thought on the part of the fibber and you're more likely to catch them in a lie than if you ask questions that only require a yes or no answer.

After you've been through the whole story, change the subject and act like you're satisfied with what you've been told. If possible, leave it alone for a day or two before broaching the subject again. Ask the person to retell the story and listen for glaring inconsistencies. After a couple days, or even a couple hours, lies start to fade from memory. A person who has fabricated a story is going to have a tough time putting the story in the same sequence they told it before.

Try asking questions that force them to jump around in the story. This will really tax their memory. Another trick that works well is to partially answer questions for them, but answer them incorrectly. "Now you said that you . . ." followed by something that doesn't jive with what you were told previously is going to get corrected by someone pulling facts from memory. A person who's struggling to remember the lies they told might agree with you because their memory of the lies is hazy.

When you have someone on the hot seat, you can really toy with their emotions in order to tell if they're lying about something. Start pressing them a bit about the topic you think they're lying about. Right in the middle of questioning, change the subject to something completely unrelated and watch their reaction closely. A guilty person is going to be relieved that the subject changed. They'll jump right to the new subject without pause. A person who is rightfully proclaiming their innocence will be surprised by this tactic and will appear confused. Try switching back and forth a couple more times and watch their reaction.

It's important not to be too aggressive during questioning. You can cause someone to permanently clam up if you push too hard. Try to befriend them instead and try to elicit a confession. Telling them you're on their side and you think you may be able to work through it is more likely to get the truth than taking a hard line right from the beginning.

Learn to trust your gut, but accept that you might be wrong. If you suspect someone is lying, but can't get

enough evidence to pursue it, your only option may be to let it go and keep a close eye on the person you suspect is lying.

Dishonest people rarely only tell one lie. You'll have plenty of opportunity to catch them lying later on down the road.

3.4: Identifying an Online Liar

Ah, the Internet. For some, it's a playground full of interesting and wonderful things. For others, it's a scary place full of deception and deceit. While the Internet offers a world of information and fun, there are a number of characters lurking in the shadows, just waiting for an innocent victim to fall into their lap.

And fall they do. Anywhere that there's human interaction online, there's people pretending to be something they're not, hoping to be able to lure someone away from the herd in order to take advantage of them.

According to the *2011 Internet Crime Report* issued by the Internet Crime Complaint Center (IC3), 314,246 complaints were lodged in 2011 alone, with over $485 million dollars having been lost to fraud. The average amount lost for those who reported a loss was more than $4,000. Over 26,000 complaints were lodged every month in 2011 with the IC3 alone. Keep in mind that the IC3 is a United States-based agency and primarily deals with crimes reported or committed in the U.S. Also keep in mind that a large percentage of fraud goes unreported.

When it comes to deception on the Internet, reported fraud is only the tip of the iceberg.

From people hiding behind fake usernames in chat rooms and forums to people filling their online dating profiles full of lies, the Internet is rife with deception. Often, this deception can take an emotional toll as well as a financial one. Scams involving romance are particularly troubling because they prey on people's emotions. Not only are the victims left with an empty wallet, they're also left with an empty heart and a badly bruised psyche.

Scammers have no problem pretending to be something they aren't on online dating sites in order to lure in hopeless romantics searching for love. They'll profess their love for someone and slowly but surely reel them in—then they hit them with it. Something bad has happened and they need money. The scammers tell their "lovers" that they're in financial trouble and need money to make it through some sort of hardship. All too often, the money is sent and the recipient disappears, never to be heard from again. In other cases, the scammer continues milking the victim for as much as they can get from them. It isn't unheard of for victims to wind up penniless—and alone.

The *2011 Internet Crime Report* reports $50.4 million in losses due to romantic scams in 2011 at an average cost of $8,900 per victim. Almost $6,000 an hour is lost to romantic scamming. What is reported is only a small amount of the scams that have actually been committed.

Victims of romantic scams are often scared to come forward out of fear of ridicule and because they're ashamed to admit they fell in love with someone who wasn't the person they thought they were. A number of them are also left believing they've somehow done something to upset their lover and are hoping against hope the person will return to them in the future. They don't realize they've been scammed; they think the lover broke things off because of a fight or for some other reason.

While there are so many online scams that it would be impossible to list them all, there are some things you can do to identify online liars well in advance of falling victim to them:

- **Don't believe everything you see or hear online.** Just because it's printed on a web site doesn't make it automatically true. If something sounds too good to be true, it probably is. Investigate everything. A good place to start when it comes to businesses is:

    http://www.ripoffreport.com/

- **You can also check snopes.com to verify the truth of any e-mails or chain messages you get to see whether they're true or not.** Snopes has a huge database debunking many of the Internet myths and scams being passed around.
- **Don't trust e-mail from anyone you don't recognize.** Just because an e-mail says it's from the FBI, the U.S. government or a popular online storefront or payment service doesn't mean it actually is. Send all spam straight to the trash heap. *Phishing scams* are scams in which scammers pretend to represent a popular site in order to get you to enter your username, password and/or credit card information. An e-mail is sent out asking you to update your information or telling you some sort of fraud is suspected. The e-mail provides a link that takes you to a site that looks exactly like the site of the company the scammer is claiming to represent. When you enter your information, it's

delivered right into the hands of the scammer and it now can be used to steal your account information, make illegal purchases and to steal your identity. If you get an e-mail asking for personal information, call the company that sent the e-mail to verify. Don't call the number in the e-mail—it could be a fake number the scammer has set up to trick you into entering your info.

- **Don't trust e-mail from people you do recognize.** Hackers have been known to infect computers with viruses capable of opening an infected person's address book and sending e-mail messages to everyone in the address book. The e-mail looks like it came from the person who's been infected, so people are more likely to trust that it's legitimate. Personal correspondences between friends is OK, but never send your personal information to your friends over the Internet.
- **Don't open attachments sent in e-mails.** Viruses can be attached to e-mails. If you get an e-mail with an attachment, don't open the attachment unless it's something you've been expecting from a friend. Even then, you should scan it using an anti-virus program before opening it.
- **Monitor you credit and bank statements for signs of fraud.** Criminals don't always hit your bank account with multiple big purchases. Sometimes you're hit with small amounts being pulled out every month. Over time, it adds up to big dollars. Check your statement regularly to make sure you aren't being bled dry.

- **Don't trust that people are who they say they are.** This is a big one, especially in the online dating arena. If you're looking for your perfect match online, you need to exercise extreme caution. Avoid long-distance relationships and never send money to someone you haven't met. If you agree to meet someone in person, set the initial meeting up so it's in a public place where you'll be able to get away quickly if the person turns out not to be who they say they are. If you're starting to get serious about someone, you might want to run a background check on them to see exactly what you're dealing with. Trust your intuition. If something doesn't feel right, it probably isn't. Don't walk right into potentially dangerous situations.
- **Make purchases from trusted sites that guarantee against fraud.** Most of the major sites guarantee you'll get the items you're paying for. You're generally safe using these sites because they'll reimburse you if someone takes off with your money. Paypal offers protection for buyers who use their service to make qualified purchases, so you're relatively safe with them as well. Make sure you read the terms of service for any storefront, auction site or payment service that you use so you'll know what is and what isn't protected. Don't fall for scams that try to steer you away from the protection of the site. Unscrupulous sellers may offer to sell you an item for less if you send them cash or a check so they can avoid the site fees. Not only is this against the terms of service of most sites, it's almost always

a scam. You'll lose your money, and you'll lose it in a place where you probably aren't going to get reimbursed.
- **Great deals can be found on classified ad sites like Craigslist, but you usually aren't protected against fraud.** If you get ripped off, you're going to lose your money. Make sure you have the product in hand before paying for it. It's important to set up your meeting in a public place. I've heard stories of people asking to meet in a police station parking lot or even in the lobby of the local police station. You're almost guaranteed a safe transaction if you go that route. One more tip . . . Always open the box before paying. It's not unheard of for a scammer to get an empty product box and put something heavy in it so the box feels like it's full. When you get home and open it, you'll find a brick or a rock. When you consider the cost of a new iPad or television, you could potentially end up paying $500 or more for something you could find for free in the nearest field.
- **Liars are more talkative.** Instead of providing simple yes or no answers, they'll try to explain everything.
- **If you're buying a house or a car, verify that the seller actually owns the house or car that they're selling.** Scammers have been known to list vehicles and houses they don't own. They'll list desirable items for ridiculously low prices and will have a number of excuses as to why they can't show them to you. Always make sure the seller owns the items

they're selling you or you may end up spending tens or even hundreds of thousands of dollars for something that belongs to someone else.
- **Don't let your offline trust bias carry over into your online interactions.** Trust nobody online. Nobody. Be careful when dealing with people within your country. Be even more careful when dealing with people from a different country. It helps to remember that other countries don't have the same consumer protection laws in place and it'll be nigh on impossible to track a fraudster from another country down to prosecute them.
- **Cash, wire transfers and businesses that operate out of a P.O. box are all a big no-no.** Reputable businesses accept credit cards or Paypal. Never pay cash or make a wire transfer if you don't have the product in hand.
- **Watch for people who don't refer to themselves in first person.** If you're talking to someone and they use the word "I" a lot, they're more likely to be telling the truth about who they are if they refer to themselves in third person or drop the "I."

In the event you find yourself a victim of online fraud or if you believe someone is trying to make a victim of you, report it immediately to IC3. Here's a link to their website:

http://www.ic3.gov/default.aspx

Be aware that there are people telling lies online for reasons other than defrauding you of your money.

Predators troll chat rooms and social networking sites looking for easy marks they can rob, rape or kill. Don't give out your personal information online and don't assume people are who they say they are. That cute 15-year old boy chatting it up with your daughter could be a 36-year old ex-felon looking to lure a young girl into his clutches.

The Online Dating Dilemma

Dating services are especially bad when it comes to people telling lies. The deception runs the gamut from people bending the truth a bit about their weight and financial information to people who flat-out lie and use fake profile photos.

Jennifer Wells fell for one of these fraudsters when she first dipped her toes in the online dating pool. No sooner had she signed up for the site than she had a private message pop into her in-box from an attractive young man claiming to be interested in her. His profile picture showed a muscular man with his shirt off at the beach. He was in good shape and looked good. His profile indicated he had a good job and owned his own house in the suburbs.

Wow, thought Jennifer, *it didn't take long to attract a winner*.

A few e-mails were sent back and forth and phone numbers were soon exchanged. After a handful of phone calls, Jennifer agreed to meet her suitor at his house after work and they were to head out for a night on the town once he was done getting ready.

Imagine Jennifer's surprise when she arrived at her date's house to find it was in a rundown part of town. It didn't really look like the house in the picture online, but she couldn't say for sure that it wasn't. A man much older than the one in the profile picture opened the door and invited her in. Something didn't feel right, but she went in anyway.

The man closed and locked the door behind Jennifer and told her to have a seat on the couch. He then revealed that he was the person who she'd been chatting with and begged her not to be upset with him for misrepresenting himself. He said he'd seen her picture and thought she was beautiful and had created a fake profile on the spot so he could attract her interest.

Jennifer was thoroughly creeped out at this point and got up to leave. The man pushed her back down onto the couch and professed his undying love for her. She got up again and was pushed back down onto the couch with even more force. Jennifer reached into her purse and pulled out a can of pepper spray, threatening to spray the man in his face if he didn't let her leave. He allowed her to get up and go, begging her not to leave him the entire time.

Jennifer got lucky. Many people don't.

She violated a number of online dating rules and almost paid a steep price for it. If you do decide to venture into the world of online dating, here are some rules you need to follow in order to stay safe:

- **Double check to make sure a person is who they say they are.** Talk to them for a while, and then ask them pointed questions about where they work and where they live. It wouldn't hurt to call their place of work and ask to speak to them before you meet them in person. If you find out no one there knows who the person is, you've just identified an online dating site liar. Break things off immediately and try again.

- **Always meet in a public place.** If the person is a creep or isn't who you thought they were going to be you can make a hasty retreat without having to escape their clutches. Meet in a public place full of people like a coffee shop or a restaurant. A person who isn't looking to get you alone so they can take advantage of you should have no problem with this.
- **Ask for additional pictures.** People have been known to steal an attractive picture from somewhere on the Internet and act like they're that person. By asking for additional pictures, you're double checking to make sure the person is who they say they are. If they aren't able to provide additional pictures, they're probably not the person in the profile. Better yet, ask for a picture of the person doing something out of the ordinary. Tell them you want to make sure they are who they say they are and ask for a picture of them covering their eyes or doing something people don't normally do in pictures.
- **Look for words that mean something else.** Know the online dating lingo. A person who says he's "cuddly" or like "a giant teddy bear" is probably overweight. Most people won't come out and tell you they're 50 pounds overweight or that they have a large lump on their neck. They may allude to it, so you have to be able to read between the lines. When

in doubt, ask. You're looking for the perfect partner, and you deserve an honest answer.

- **Don't go straight from messaging to the first date.** Some people might have someone else help them write the messages so they sound smarter or wittier. A phone call will reveal a lot about a person. Sure, they could have someone else field the call as well, but calls aren't as easy to fake as text. When in doubt, ask the person to meet you in a video chat room or to use video conferencing on a smart phone. That way, you can make sure you're talking to the person you think you are.

- **Don't tell potential dates where you live or give them too much of your personal information.** If you're interested in someone, all you really need to tell them is your first name. You can reveal more about yourself if the first date goes well. A stalker with your last name may be able to look you up online.

- **Don't trust profile information.** Most people exaggerate on their profile. They want to put their best foot forward. A little bit of exaggeration isn't a big deal. Everybody does it. What is a big deal are lies. If a person tells you they have a job and a house and it turns out they're unemployed and live in their mother's basement, that's should be enough to warrant you moving on to someone else. Profile photos can also be faked or exaggerated. People want to put their best foot forward and will use an old picture that makes them look younger and in better shape than they are now.

- **Don't send money to someone you haven't met—or have met and don't know that well.** Scammers are willing to spend a lot of time wooing you and convincing you they're falling deeply in love. Once you're in love, they hit you with it. They call up with a story of how they're in deep trouble and need your help. They're smart enough not to ask you for money—they wait for you to offer it a reluctantly accept. Guess what? You've just been played. You either won't hear from that person again or you will and they'll need more money. People have been milked for their entire life savings by "lovers" claiming distress. If you suspect you're being taken advantage of, tell the person you'd love to help them, but you aren't able to and watch how fast they disappear.

The best thing you can do is to use a little common sense. Look at everything objectively and don't let your vision get clouded by thoughts of everlasting love. That's what the con artists are counting on—and that's the reason why there's so many of them prowling the online dating sites and chat rooms.

Exercise caution and you might meet the man or woman of your dreams. Let your emotions take control and you might meet financial ruin or worse.

Chapter 4: The Best Defense against Lies and Those Who Tell Them

"Tricks and treachery are the practice of fools, that don't have brains enough to be honest."

-Benjamin Franklin

Odds are you're going to be told a lie today. There may be lies told about you. The more popular or famous you are, the more detractors you're going to have. If you're in a position of power, you have to be ready for those who will look to defame you by doing whatever it takes—up to and including lying.

The best defense is to strike preemptively by always carrying yourself with integrity. Answer questions openly and honestly and don't place yourself in a position where lies can take you down.

When a person tells a lie about someone, they do it in order to assassinate that person's character. You can make yourself bulletproof by being a person of such high moral value that others won't believe attempts to assassinate your character. You'll be innocent until proven guilty.

On the other hand, if you've been caught lying in the past, people are going to assume you're capable of lying again. You'll be guilty until proven innocent. You can deny the false allegations, but people will automatically assume you're lying again. They're going to require proof, and lots of it. Even if you're able to disprove the lies being told, the damage will have been done.

If you make a mistake, own up to it. If you do something wrong and are caught, admit you were wrong and apologize. Doing so will place you in a position where you'll be able to discredit liars and have people believe what you tell them.

The best defense against lies and the people who tell them is to be honest, even when being honest is to your detriment.

4.1: The Only Way You Can Be Lied to Is If You Let it Happen

When I first tell people that the only way they can be lied to is if they let it happen I get a lot of blank stares. It's difficult to fathom how a person would *let* someone lie to them. Someone invariably chimes in that they don't *allow* people to lie to them, they just do.

While it's true that people will *try* to lie to you no matter what you do, that doesn't mean you *have to* believe everything you're told. The only way a lie is successful is if you believe it. You're 100% percent in control of what you believe and what you don't believe.

It takes two to tango when it comes to lies. The liar tells the lie and the person being lied to believes it. You can't stop the liars from lying, but you can make changes on your end so you don't complete the lie.

The only way a liar can successfully tell a lie is if you fall for it. Instead of believing everything you're told, closely examine what you're being told.

If someone tells you they have a great deal on real estate in Wyoming and it piques your interest, don't automatically assume they're telling the truth. Question their motives. If they have a great deal, why aren't they taking advantage of it? What do they have to gain by passing the deal on to you? Is the person your friend or just someone you know? How likely is it you're being lied to?

Next, assess what you've been told to see if it makes sense. Where is the real estate in Wyoming? What makes it such a great deal? Is it in a rapidly growing area where property values are increasing or is it in the wilderness where the value isn't likely to change much? Is the property being sold at well below market value? Why is it being sold at the price it's listed for? Is this deal on the up and up?

Discovering the truth behind a statement requires assessing it from all angles to make sure everything adds up. Don't make any assumptions because assumptions invariably end up costing you in the long run. Arm yourself with facts that you know are accurate and you'll be much less likely to be able to be lied to.

Don't be afraid to put off making a decision on something you aren't sure about until a later date.

High-pressure salesmen and con artists try to push people into making rash, on-the-spot decisions before they have a chance to think things through and verify facts. They'll tell you they have the lowest prices in town even though they're charging thousands more than the next guy.

Another tactic used by liars is to try to befriend you and act like they're the nice guy. They know you're more likely to trust someone you like, so they ply you with kind words and fill your head with happy thoughts. I've seen people pay as much as a couple thousand more dollars than they needed to on cars just because they liked the salesman and were tricked into trusting him. When they got home and starting shopping around, they found they'd been had.

Don't fall for the nice guy act. Liars aren't always creepy little rats with beady eyes. The best liars are charismatic people who light up the room when they walk in. They're capable of smiling in your face while they slip a knife into your back, all without you realizing you've been stabbed until it's too late.

Don't allow the liars to lie to you. Make it as hard as possible for them to get away with their lies. This alone will be enough to drive most liars away. Don't allow yourself to be lied to. Makes sense now, doesn't it?

Chapter 5: The Many Faces of a Liar

"Eyes show lies."

— Toba Beta, *My Ancestor Was an Ancient Astronaut*

Liars can teach themselves to hide the verbal cues and words associated with lying. They can train themselves to talk like an honest person talks.

What they more often than not can't do is hide the body language they display while engaging in lies. They know they're lying and their body reacts differently in a number of small, but usually obvious ways.

The mannerisms of a liar can tell you a lot.

Whenever you're talking to someone, watch them closely and try to establish a baseline behavior. Watch their hands, feet, legs, arms, face and head and take note of the way they're positioned and any unconscious movements or facial expressions the person makes. Once you've established a baseline, catching the speaker in a lie becomes easier because you can watch for deviations from the baseline that may be indicative of a lie.

For example, a person who looks you in the eyes while they're telling the truth may start glancing away and avoiding eye contact when they're lying. On the other hand, a person who avoids eye contact when they're telling the truth may attempt to make more eye contact when they're being deceptive. Whether or not eye contact is made isn't the determining factor in whether a person is lying or not. The idea that a liar will be afraid to make eye contact is nothing more than a wives tale. Changes in the amount of eye contact being made indicate deception, not failure to make contact at all.

While we're on the topic of eyes, watch for a person you suspect of lying to reach up and touch their eyes when being dishonest. This subconscious reaction to lying is something most people don't realize they're doing. They may rub their eyes, scratch around the edges of them or play with their eyelashes. Children are even less controlled and may completely cover their eyes with their hands, a blanket or anything else that's nearby. They may also hide behind something so they can't see you and you can't see them.

Another area liars reach up and touch when they're lying is their mouth. Children will cover their mouth as if they're ashamed that a lie has spouted forth from it. Adults are a little more refined. They may touch their mouth, run their tongue over their teeth or excessively lick their lips while lying.

Watch for what I like to call the *fake-out*. A person will begin to reach for their mouth or eyes and at the last moment will put their hand down or touch something else. This happens when a person subconsciously realizes they may be giving themselves away by touching their mouth or eyes and veers their hand off before it touches down.

One of the best ways to tell a person is lying by looking at their face is to watch the way they smile. A fake smile is a dead giveaway as to whether a person is being sincere or not. Very few people can force out a fake smile that's convincing enough to fool the experts. The key is to watch the eyes. *Laugh lines*, which are the tiny wrinkles that appear at the corners of a person's eyes when they have a genuine smile going, are the best indicator of whether a smile is real or not. With a real smile, the upper eyelid will pull down a bit, causing the laugh lines to deepen. A fake smile only uses the lips and looks forced. A real smile engages the entire face.

Another way to tell whether a smile is real or not is to watch the edges of their lips. If one side pulls higher than the other, the person doing the smiling may be feeling some emotion other than happiness. Forced smiles are rarely symmetrical. Real smiles are.

A good liar is able to display a poker face with little to no emotion being displayed whether or not lies are forthcoming. What good liars aren't able to control are the small flashes of expression they display while talking.

These brief displays of emotion are called *micro-expressions* and they're almost impossible to control.

Micro-expressions were first identified in the 1960's by a man named William Condon who spent countless hours studying video of people's facial expressions frame-by-frame. Micro-expressions are fleeting tics, smiles, lips curls, twitches and wrinkles of various parts of the face. They happen in a split second and are involuntary movements of the facial muscles that are impossible to suppress. Watch for an increase in the amount of micro-expressions or a change in the type of micro-expressions a person is displaying. A single twitch or tic may not mean anything, but identifying a series of micro-expressions combined with other verbal and physical cues will give you a pretty good chance of identifying when you're being lied to.

The direction a person looks or glances while they're talking or recalling a memory can also clue you in as to whether they're lying or not. A right-handed person may glance to the left when creating a lie. A left-handed person may look in the opposite direction, to the right. The mileage you get from this technique may vary. Some people swear by it, while others say it doesn't work. I've found it to be very telling with some people; not as much with others. Going back to baselines, if a person who normally looks straight ahead or glances to the right while he talks suddenly starts glancing left, you may be onto something. If the person glances left the entire time he's speaking, it's probably just habit and nothing to be concerned with.

Keep an eye on your subject's head while they're talking. Subtle head nods or shakes may give away their true emotions. A subtle headshake from side while a person is agreeing with you may indicate they aren't actually in agreement with what you're saying.

Yet another thing to watch out for is feigned expressions. With the exception of humor, most real emotions only last a few seconds in a normal conversation. A person pretending to feel an emotion may hold an expression on their face for 5 seconds or more in an attempt to make it look more genuine. Whenever you think a person may be faking an emotion watch for "leaks" to show through. The real emotion the person is feeling may show through via bursts of micro-expressions. You may also see another feeling start to show through the feeling a person is trying to display. If you tell an employee of yours she's been talking on her cell phone too often and she smiles and tells you she didn't realize it was problem, you may be able to see right through her smile. That's because the smile is forced and the anger she's really feeling is threatening to show through.

Be aware that even the experts aren't able to determine when a person is lying every single time they lie. You won't be able to either.

A micro-expression of fear when you ask someone a question about something may indicate they're lying—or it might just be that they're scared you'll be mad when they tell you the truth. Facial expressions are only one part of the puzzle and shouldn't be used as the sole determinant of whether you believe someone or not.

When in doubt, opt for watching the eyes over the mouth. It's difficult to reign in micro-expressions and tics of the muscles surrounding the eyes. Most people have an easier time controlling the muscles around their mouth than they do their eyes. When you start a conversation, set a baseline for the blink rate of the person you're talking to. Watch how often they blink throughout the conversation. If the frequency at which the speaker blinks speeds up at any point during the conversation, pay close attention. Increases in a person's blink rate indicate the person is nervous about something. Another indicator of raw nerves is the pupils of the eyes. Dilated pupils indicate underlying emotional turmoil.

Chapter 6: The Body Rarely Lies

"I'm bilingual, speaking English and body language. I prefer the latter, because I can speak it silently and without listening and while my back is turned."

- Jarod Kintz

Depending on the source, it's estimated that anywhere from 50% to more than 90% of communication is done non-verbally. What this means is our bodies are conveying more about the way we feel than our words are—and we're less conscious of what our bodies are doing. Liars are practiced in deception using spoken words. They aren't as adept at lying with their bodies.

Body language can tell you quite a bit about what a person is thinking.

Dishonest people are able to choose their words carefully, so as not to reveal their true feelings or intent. It isn't as easy for them to choose their body language. The average person doesn't have a clue as to what his or her body language is revealing about their inner thoughts and emotions. Even if they do know how to read body language, hiding it is a completely different story. Most people can't read body language, so even the most adept of liars can usually skate by without having to change what they're doing with their bodies.

A person who is lying is already firing on all cylinders trying to log and remember the lies they're telling. They've got to make a conscious effort not to get crossed up and make a statement that contradicts something they've already said. A person who is telling the truth doesn't have this problem because they're pulling what they're saying from memory. It takes a lot more thought and effort to tell a lie than it does the truth.

For this reason, a liar has a tough time covering up facial expressions and body language while lying. It's usually too much to focus on keeping lies straight, remembering them, suppressing facial expressions *and* remembering to control what they're saying with their body. Since most people don't know the first thing about body language, this is the first thing experienced liars let slide.

When a liar consciously tries to suppress or change their body language so it matches the words being spoken movements will be stiff and robotic. Look for changes in the fluidity of body language.

Honest body language flows in and out as part of the conversation. Forced body language looks out of place and often trails what's being said. A truly happy person who is telling you how happy they are will be smiling and displaying happy body language while they're talking. A person lying about how happy they are may tell you they're happy and then show the emotion with their body moments later. Delayed body language that lasts longer than it normally would and disappears abruptly indicates body language that's consciously being displayed, most likely because the person displaying it is trying to deceive you. Body language that's in tune with what's being said is more likely to be genuine.

Palms facing out or up indicate honesty. Politicians are trained to do this to appear as if they're more humble and are being honest. A person who isn't a politician may do this while telling the truth. If you accuse somebody at work of stealing your lunch from the fridge and they turn their palms out or up so you can see them when they answer, they're more likely to be telling the truth than if they show you the back of their hands. If they show you their fist and you see it rapidly moving toward your face, duck. You're about to get punched.

A palms-up display tells you a person is trying to submit to you and is being open and honest. Palms-down means the person is closing themselves off. A person who moves their hands behind their back or in their pockets probably has something to hide.

Watch for the barriers being placed between you and the person you're talking to. If you're talking to someone and they move so that a desk or table is between you and them, they're trying to place a barrier between the two of you. This is a hold-over from childhood. Whenever a child feels threatened or nervous they hide behind one of their parents. As adults, this desire to hide from threats manifests itself as placing a barrier. If no barrier is present, a person who feels threatened or unsure will cross their arms tightly against their chest. This creates a barrier that protects the most important part of their body: the heart.

Confront a liar out in the open and watch him squirm. A person who tells lies is going to want the comfort of a barrier. They may not confess to lying while exposed in the open, but they're more likely to than if you let them place a barrier between you and them.

When a person doesn't agree with what's being said, they will take a defensive posture with their arms folded across their chest. Folded arms indicate a negative attitude toward either the person speaking or what's being said. If a person is agreeing with you verbally and suddenly folds their arms, they're probably only agreeing with you because they don't want a confrontation. If they're tightly gripping their crossed arms, that's even worse. They have some sort of inner turmoil going on and are fighting the urge to uncross their arms.

A person who has his hands clasped together tightly is in a negative mood. This may be because the person is lying and doesn't feel good about it. It may not. It's something to watch for that doesn't mean much on its own, but can be significant when other factors are taken into consideration.

The hips, legs and feet are the most unregulated parts of the body. A person may be able to control hand gestures while talking. Hips, legs and feet are a different story. Watch for any of the three to be pointing toward an exit. A person whose head is facing you, but their hips, legs or feet are pointing toward an exit is usually wishing they could get away. They don't want to be in the conversation anymore and are hoping for a way out. If they're engaged in the conversation and are interested in it, they'll be facing you with their entire body. Their feet will be pointed at you along with their legs and hips. If an uncomfortable topic is broached, you might see part of their body shift so it's pointing toward an exit.

Reading body language is fun once you know what to look for. The key to successfully reading a person's body language is to watch for combinations of body language signals that tell you what a person is thinking. Just like we speak in sentences that are combinations of words, our body speaks in combinations of actions.

A single action that doesn't jive with what's being said probably isn't anything to worry about. An entire series of actions that don't match indicates there's something wrong.

Take a series of gestures that indicate nervousness or fear and combine them with verbal and facial cues and you'll have a pretty good idea when you're being lied to. When everything you're seeing tells you you're being lied to, assume you're being lied to and push for the truth.

Here's a nifty trick you can use to tell when someone is being less than honest. Watch for them to go completely still. Our bodies are constantly in motion when we talk. Stillness indicates an attempt to suppress all body language in order to avoid exposing a lie through incongruent body motions. A person who is normally animated may go unnaturally still when they're lying. If this happens, it's a dead giveaway.

The tendency for a person to suddenly go still is probably a throw-back to the days when our ancestors had to worry about becoming an easy meal to predators. In nature, when a helpless animal senses imminent danger they will sometimes freeze and remain completely motionless. Going motionless while lying may be a built-in defense mechanism that's ingrained into human nature.

Chapter 7: Protecting Yourself from Character Assassination

"Be more concerned with your character than your reputation, because your character is what you really are, while your reputation is merely what others think you are."

-John Wooden

***Character assassination* takes place when a person attempts to wreck another person's reputation by any means necessary.**

This includes exaggerating the facts, making up stories and bending the truth to suit their needs. A character assassin has no qualms with misleading people into believing the person they're trying to defame is a vile, disgusting human capable of all sorts of evil acts.

Character assassination is often done by telling only part of a story or spinning a story to make it sound worse than it is in an attempt to demonize the victim in the eyes of others. The assassin does so while feigning they're taking the moral high ground by exposing the victim's evil deeds. This puts them at an advantage in multiple ways. They position themselves as a person willing to tell the "truth" no matter what the cost and they invoke moral outrage toward the victim.

The effects of a targeted character assassination can be devastating to an individual. The damage done can last for years and in some cases is impossible to reverse.

Once people form an opinion of you, it's tough to reverse that opinion. You might find yourself ostracized from your family, your friends and even your community. You may be passed over for promotions at work or even terminated because your place of employment doesn't want to be associated with someone who acts in the manner you've been accused of acting. Entire careers have been ruined in a heartbeat by character assassination campaigns.

If you watch TV when an important election is pending, you'll see all sorts of attempts at character assassination. Campaign ads make all sorts of claims about candidates and smear campaigns are an accepted political tactic. While politicians don't usually directly smear other politicians, all sorts of "concerned citizen" committees have ads smearing one candidate or another. Most of these ads are backed by a candidate who stands to benefit from the ad.

While politicians can hire people to fight character assassination attempts and are often coached on how to best handle a sticky situation, handling a character crisis is difficult for the rest of us. It can feel like you're walking through a minefield with all eyes on you, waiting for you to step on a mine and explode.

Your first instinct when a character assassination attempt is underway is going to be to lash out in anger. This is what the assassin is hoping you'll do.

By reacting angrily, you're confirming the fact that you're not a good person. If you lash out violently, that's even worse. You're just proving the assassin's point and making his job easier. You'll now be painted as a loose cannon ready to go off half-cocked and as a danger to yourself and those around you.

You may be tempted to ignore the assassination attempt in in hope it will go away. The problem with ignoring something of this magnitude is that it's only going to get bigger. Once a fire's been lit, silence on your part adds fuel to it. People will start to talk and a small flame can quickly turn into a raging wildfire.

You're going to be embarrassed by the rumors spread about you, even if there's only a speck of truth to them. Your first instinct might be to hide yourself out of sight until the storm has passed. This is a bad idea because people will think you're hiding from the truth and are scared to face the music. Tucking yourself away out of sight confirms people's suspicions about you.

Hide yourself away at the first sign of trouble and you may end up a recluse, banished to your home by a community that distrusts and dislikes you.

Carry on with life like you normally would, ignoring the whispers and sideways glances. You know the rumors aren't true. Act like you expect everyone else not to believe them either.

The best course of action is to confront the issue head-on. If you're being accused of something illegal that could potentially send you to jail or cost you money in a civil suit, your best bet is to hire a lawyer immediately and let him advise you as to the best course of action. You don't want to make a mistake that costs you dearly later on down the road. When your freedom and financial security are on the line, you don't want to take advice from a book. You want the advice of a professional who's well-versed in the laws in your jurisdiction.

If the issue is a minor one that only threatens to damage your reputation, you might decide to handle it yourself. The key to handling a potentially damaging situation successfully is to stay calm and carry yourself with poise.

Directly confronting the person spreading the rumors may be the best course of action.

Never do so alone. You could be accused of any number of things you didn't say or do. A manager unjustly accused of sexual harassment isn't going to do himself any favors by confronting the person who is making the accusations alone. All that does is open him up to the potential of even more accusations being levied. He may find he's now accused of harassment and threatening the person making the accusations—and he'll be powerless to deny it because no one witnessed the meeting.

If you are going to confront someone about rumors they've been spreading about you, you're going to want to do so in person and with witnesses present. At work, you're going to want to have management or representatives from HR present to oversee the meeting. If the accusations could later result in legal action being taken, you may also want to have a lawyer along. What you say can and will be held against you. It helps to remember that nothing you say at work will be off the record. Slip up and it could tarnish your record permanently.

Sometimes, all it takes is you standing up for yourself and definitively stating a person is lying and trying to assassinate your character to get them to stop. An inexperienced character assassin will more often than not be scared off by you simply confronting them head-on.

Remember, always have witnesses present and always carry yourself calmly and confidently. Tell the person you're confronting that you've heard they've been spreading rumors about you and you want to know what they've been telling people. If they refuse to admit they've been talking behind your back, state exactly what it is you've heard from other people and ask them point blank whether they've been spreading the rumors or not. It's important to be very clear about what you've heard they've been telling people.

It helps if one of the people who have been told the rumor is present and willing to speak up because the assassin may try to say he hasn't been spreading rumors. Having one of the people who were told the rumor at the meeting eliminates this escape route.

Once you've got the accusations out in the open, it's time to let the person know what you expect of them in the future. Tell them how you want the problem resolved. Tell them you want them to stop spreading the rumor immediately and lay out the consequences if they continue to spread rumors behind your back. Don't threaten to do them harm; instead threaten legal action or threaten to out their lies publicly. If you're at work, it will be up to management or HR what the repercussions will be. You need to make it clear that you want the rumors to stop. Let the powers that be decide what the punishment for failing to stop spreading them will be.

There may be times when lies are told about you and you aren't able to accurately identify the source. When this happens, you have to identify all of the potential sources and ask them to stop spreading rumors.

One person leads to another person leads to another and nobody will fess up to being the person who started the rumor. In this case, you need to let everyone you can identify as potential sources of the rumor know that it's false and ask that they stop propagating it.

For a rumor making its rounds at work, go straight to your boss. Let your boss know what you've heard and tell him or her it isn't true. Don't worry about broaching the subject with your boss; chances are they've heard the rumor already. By confronting it directly, you're letting them know you didn't do what you're being accused of and are concerned enough about it to call a meeting with them. They should be able to respect that—unless they're the ones spreading the rumor. Even then, it should make them take pause. If you're willing to go to them, they'll realize you're more than capable of going over their head.

One last thing on character assassination—attempts to assassinate your character are rarely as bad as they first seem. You may be devastated by what you've heard and think that people are going to look at you differently for the rest of your life. While this may be the case if you've been accused of rape, murder or child molestation and people believe, most other attempts to assassinate your character will eventually be forgotten.

Put an end to any attempt to assassinate your character, set the record straight and carry on with your life.

Chapter 8: Stop Lying to Yourself

"Above all, don't lie to yourself. The man who lies to himself and listens to his own lie comes to a point that he cannot distinguish the truth within him, or around him, and so loses all respect for himself and for others."

— Fyodor Dostoyevsky, *The Brothers Karamazov*

I want to start this chapter by telling you you're probably not going to like what you're about to hear. You're going to want to discount what you're being told and won't want to admit that you lie to yourself. If you take the contents of this chapter to heart, it could be the most important chapter of any book you read in your entire life . . . But you have to take it to heart and take action. Don't just read it and go "Yeah, I do lie to myself" and go back to your daily life.

The main thing holding most of us back from becoming the person we could potentially be is the fact that we're able to unapologetically lie to ourselves. We lie to ourselves about how happy we are, what we want out of life, what direction our life is headed in and why we do the things we do.

While we hate being lied to by others, we tell ourselves lie after lie and feel no remorse.

We tell ourselves we don't have time to the do the important things we know we should be doing while wasting time on inconsequential tasks. The Internet is the biggest time-sucker on the planet. Sure, it has its uses, but do you really need to spend an hour a day catching up with people you went to high school with on Facebook and pinning stuff to your many Pinterest boards? Just think of how much healthier you'd be if you spent that time working out or working toward starting your own business or doing something else constructive.

We've even got a word for lying to ourselves that makes it seem like something that's OK to do. The word is *rationalizing.* If you find yourself spending more time thinking about reasons why you can't do something important than reasons why you can, you're lying to yourself. Call it rationalizing if you want, but it all boils down to one thing.

You don't want to change, so you're lying to yourself in order to avoid having to change.

The problem with this line of thinking is we usually lie to ourselves to avoid doing things we know we should be doing, but don't want to. Working out takes time, so we convince ourselves we don't have a half hour a day to work out. We convince ourselves eating right takes time and money that we don't have, so we gorge ourselves on junk food and hit the drive-thru when it's time for dinner. We convince ourselves we don't have time to take a class or two after work, so we end up stuck in a dead end job. We don't want to clean, so we find a thousand reasons not to.

Lying to yourself is almost always destructive. It prevents you from achieving your goals and, at best, it stagnates your efforts to move ahead in life. You end up old, poor and unhealthy, all because of the lies you've been telling yourself.

You know what you're supposed to be doing, so stop lying to yourself and get out there and do it.

If you don't have time, find time. There are CEOs who work 15 hours days who manage to find time to work out. You can squeeze in a quick workout between taking the kids to soccer practice and dinner.

Don't allow your subconscious mind to convince your conscious self that you're incapable of change. Commit to stop lying to yourself and commit to constantly move forward. You'll be a better person because of it. Anything that you want is life is attainable once you stop making excuses.

You want wealth? Stop lying to yourself and telling yourself you can't do it. You can do it; you're just too scared of failure to try. Get out there and take your lumps. Learn how to make money and then start making it. It's not going to be easy and you're going to make mistakes, but no one gets rich sitting on the couch. Learn from your mistakes and carry on. You'll eventually figure it all out.

You want more time to spend with your family? Create time. Stop lying to yourself and telling yourself you're too busy. If your job keeps you away from home for days or weeks on end, start looking for a new job that doesn't. If you want to stay home with your kids, you can do that, too. You might have to learn to live with less money, but it can be done. Stop fearing change and embrace it. If you're miserable right now, there's no reason to stay the course that you're on.

You want to be healthier? Find time to work out. Find time to eat healthy. Choose Subway over McDonald's. Order a salad instead of a Big Mac. Work out at lunch time and eat a protein bar instead of hanging out with your friends. If you found out you would die if you ate another cheeseburger or another slice of pizza, would you ever eat another slice? No, but you're more than willing to kill yourself slowly.

You want to quit smoking, drinking, doing drugs or any of a number of other vices? Stop lying to yourself and telling yourself you can't. You can. You just don't because it's easier not to. If the physical addiction is too much to kick, rehab is an option, but you still have to stop lying to yourself and commit to it.

Stop lying to yourself. It can be done. There a millions of people just like you who have had the same problems and time constraints you have who have done the things you've been ignoring. Become a doer instead of a watcher.

Stop lying to yourself.

8.1: You Do Have Time

I don't have time is one of the most common rationalizations people use when lying to themselves. People use being pressed for time as an excuse for everything from not working out to not spending enough quality time with their kids.

My response to this is *make time*.

Most people aren't busy from the beginning of the day until the end of the day. If you're one of those few unfortunate people working a 12 or more hour a day job, then I feel for you. Even then, you can find time to work out, eat right and to spend more time with your kids.

The fact of the matter is most people waste time every day. Instead of lying to yourself and telling yourself you don't have time, take a close look at your life and identify where you're wasting time, then spend that time doing the things you've been putting off. Here are some of the common areas where people waste time without realizing it:

- **The Internet.** Log off and spend your time doing something more constructive. Facebook will still be there when you're done. Try rewarding yourself for being constructive with a half hour to an hour a day online.
- **Procrastination.** This is one of the biggest forms of lying to yourself. It's a sneaky one, too. One minute your heart is set on heading to the gym or cleaning the house and the next you find yourself sitting on the couch watching TV for three hours on your day off. Chronic procrastinators are able to get nothing

done by convincing themselves they'll have time to do it later. The problem is, later never comes. There's always a reason not to do something. Start finding reasons to do stuff instead of putting it off until later.
- **Video games.** Last I checked, the only people making money playing video games weren't doing so from the comfort of their own living room. Video games suck down countless hours of productive time. Put your controllers away and play games when you actually have spare time. It's OK to play games when you have free time and want to unwind. It isn't OK to play them while ignoring your other responsibilities.
- **Sleep.** Sure, you need sleep. 8 hours a day should be more than enough. You can get by with 6 when you have to. Oversleeping can actually make you more tired during the day and cut down on productivity during your waking hours.
- **TV.** This is another big time waster. If you have a favorite show you just can't bear to miss, it's probably OK to take time off each week to watch it. If you have 10 favorite shows you can't bear to miss, you're using TV as an excuse to be inactive.
- **Reading.** While a certain level of reading keeps your mind sharp, you could potentially be using reading to escape from your responsibilities. There's nothing wrong with being a bookworm if you have time, and there's something to be said about curling up with a good book; just don't let that book be the reason you don't meet your other responsibilities.

Lying to yourself and telling yourself you're just going to read another chapter has the same effect as lying to yourself and telling yourself you don't have time.

We'd all be better people leading healthier lives if we'd stop lying to ourselves.

It's time to recognize the difference between not having time and not wanting to have time. You can make time to do the things you need to do. It's going to take sacrifice in other areas of your life, but the payoff will be worth it later on down the road. You'll feel better about yourself and will know you've done everything you can to ensure you reach your maximum potential.

You don't want to grow old and look back on your life and wonder what you could have become. You want to look back and be proud of what you accomplished. You don't reach that point by lying to yourself.

8.2: Things Won't Get Any Better ... Unless You Make Them Better

Another lie people like to tell themselves is that things will get better later on down the road. Things *could* potentially get better, but they won't if you don't do something to make your dreams a reality.

While time does heal some wounds, life isn't going to get any better if you don't take the steps necessary today to reach your future goals. By constantly lying to yourself and telling yourself things are going to get better, you create a never-ending cycle where you believe things will get better and sit around waiting for it to happen. The more you sit around doing nothing, the worse things get, with you sitting right there in the middle hoping your lucky break is coming.

Sure, you might win the lottery or stumble upon the perfect job by accident, but the chances of that happening are infinitesimally small. Waiting for things to get better is a fool's game—and one you're unlikely to win. Instead of waiting for things to get better, get out there and make sure they get better. If you aren't happy with the direction your life is headed, take action to change the direction.

You're lying to yourself if you're telling yourself you want to lose weight, but haven't been to the gym in years. You're lying to yourself if you say you want to get married, but haven't been on a date since high school. You're lying to yourself if you say you want a clean house, but you sit on the couch all day watching TV.

It's time to stop lying to yourself.

Once you stop lying to yourself and start taking action, things will slowly but surely improve. You'll feel better about yourself and life in general. Instead of wallowing in self-pity and loathing yourself, you'll love yourself for having taken action and will be on the path to success.

Chapter 9: Ten Big Lies You Might Hear at Work

"I would never lie. I willfully participate in a campaign of misinformation."

—Fox Mulder, X-Files

Meghan Taylor is 29 years old. She's not old, by any means, but she feels she should be way further ahead in life than she currently is. She's a bright young woman with a Master's Degree in Business Technology and she's only worked two jobs in her field since she graduated 7 years ago.

Meghan worked the first job for 6 ½ of those years. She was a model employee; always the first to arrive and the last to leave and worked her butt off to get ahead. The problem is she never got ahead. No matter what she did, she couldn't seem to catch a break.

There were numerous promises of raises, bonuses and pending promotions, but none of them ever came to fruition. For 6 long years, Meghan chalked it up to bad luck. She figured the people who got the promotions and big raises were doing a better job than her and deserved them more than she did, even though all evidence pointed to the contrary. Her boss, Christine, had a million excuses as to why Meghan was passed over at every opportunity.

Eventually Meghan started to suspect something was up. Christine's excuses got weaker and weaker and people who'd only been working at the company for a few years were being promoted over Meghan. She quietly questioned her boss's motives, but was too timid to speak up.

One day, Meghan was asked to work on a project for the Vice President of the company. She realized this was her big chance to wow the powers that be and really busted her tail to make sure the job got done accurately and on time. The VP of Operations praised her work ethic and told her what an exemplary employee she'd been.

"You've done such a great job here," he told her. "I've got to ask. Christine says you have no desire to move up in the ranks. Why is that?"

Meghan was appalled to find out her boss had been holding her back all these years. She told the VP that she'd been trying to get promoted for years and had been lied to every time she'd been up for a promotion. The VP was shocked and called Christine to his office immediately. When Christine got there, he dressed her down and asked for an explanation. Christine acted shocked and claimed she had honestly thought Meghan didn't want to be promoted. The VP told Christine that Meghan was to be considered for the next promotion and left it at that.

Disappointed in both her boss and the VP's handling of the situation, Meghan decided to leave the company and start fresh somewhere else. She quickly found a new job and left the original company, having wasted 6 ½ years working for a boss who'd lied to her every step of the way.

While Meghan's story is extreme, most of us have been lied to by a boss at some point in our lives. It may have been because they were trying to spare our feelings or it may have been because they were pushed to lie by someone at a higher level than them. Or it may just be that the boss is a dishonest person who lies because it's easier than telling the truth.

There are a number of lies you might be told at work. The following list contains some of the more common ones:

1: There will be no bonuses or raises this year because . . .

Bonuses and raises are the first things to go when a company hits a slow period and is struggling to make ends meet. If the reason you're given doesn't involve finances, you're probably being lied to.

2: Your salary is in line with what people of your experience and skill level are making.

This is the number one excuse bosses give when they don't want to give you a raise. Do your due diligence and meet with your boss armed with the numbers and you'll be able to do a better job of pleading your case. If you truly are underpaid and your company holds a hard line, leaving may be your only option.

3: Let me talk that over with the powers that be.

When your boss tells you this one, what he's more than likely telling you is his mind is already made up and he's going to tell you no; he just doesn't want to take all of the blame for it. Expect him to come back later and try to gently let you down.

4: We've got a plan to turn things around.

If this statement is followed by details of the plan, then your company might be OK. On the other hand, if you're told this and it isn't followed up with specific details, the company either doesn't have a plan or has one that's so weak management has been told not to reveal it to employees. Time to start exploring other options.

5: This is a temp-to-hire position.

While there are indeed temporary employees that work their way into permanent positions, the odds aren't with you. Most of time, a temp-to-hire position is a temporary position that management calls temp-to-hire in order to get better people. If you're unemployed, don't avoid temporary jobs just because they're temporary; just be aware that temp-to-hire jobs rarely evolve into full-time positions.

Think of a temp job as a bridge between unemployment and finding a FT position. Try to find a temporary job that will help you build on your skills and make you more employable.

6: That's just a rumor . . .

This is one to watch closely. If the rumor you've just asked about has some truth to it, your boss will display signs of nervousness and possibly anger that you've found out through the grapevine. Rumors with no truth to them will be categorically denied. If your boss beats around the bush and won't give you a straight answer, then there's at least some truth to the rumor.

7: We're all working toward the same goal.

As long as that goal includes a big end-of-year bonus for your boss, then, yes, you're all working toward the same goal. It helps to remember that most people are more concerned with their personal advancement and goals than they are with the greater goals of the company.

8: The other person was more qualified.

Yes, the other person may have been more qualified. The other person may also have been a friend or family member of someone in management or the other person might have meshed better with the people doing the interviewing.

9: We're implementing a hiring freeze.

Read this as saying "The company's growth has stagnated. Layoffs may be coming." A hiring freeze is rarely a good thing. During the typical hiring freeze, no new workers are added and employees who quit or retire aren't replaced. This means more work for everyone else while the company teeters precariously over the abyss.

10: We're looking for volunteers.

When a company asks for volunteers, what they're really saying is they expect people to sign up. If enough volunteers fail sign up, they'll start requiring people to come in to work.

Chapter 10: What to Do When Your Kids Start Lying

"Telling lies and showing off to get attention are mistakes I made that I don't want my kids to make."

—Jane Fonda

At some point in their young lives, almost all children tell a lie. It's usually a whopper of a story, and it's often so far-fetched that it borders on the verge of hilarity. You won't know whether to discipline your child for fabricating such a story or to crack up laughing and let it slide.

Toddlers and preschoolers love to make up stories.

This really isn't lying per-se. It's them using their budding imaginations to create interesting and entertaining worlds. Unless the stories are violent or involve unacceptable accusations, it's usually OK to let them slide or even encourage them. A child with an active imagination isn't a bad thing.

As the child ages, they will invariably attempt to use a made-up story as an excuse for why they did something. This is when you need to step in and explain to the child that they can't use their imagination to get them out of trouble for something they really did. By responding immediately to a fabricated excuse for a real-world action, you're letting the child know there are limits to what they can use their imagination for. This won't completely put an end to lying later on in life, but it will lay the groundwork for your child to know right from wrong.

Pre-teens and teenagers will often go through a stage where they lie constantly and are sneaky. They're testing their boundaries and clear punishment needs to be set and enforced for lying. Allowing a teenager to get away with lying because you're frustrated and tired of arguing with her will set the stage for further lies to be told in the future. Once a teenager sees that lying is the path of least resistance, that's the path they'll take time and time again.

Lying becomes a crutch they're able to rely on when they think they're going to get in trouble. Exasperated parents who give up and accept lies from their kids are only aggravating the situation.

Telling lies is often a gateway to other more concerning behavior. Once a child learns they can get away with lying, they'll push the limits of what they can get away with. They'll start acting out and lying about it, pushing the boundaries a little further each time they act out. This can lead to lies that cover up serious issues like drug and alcohol abuse and unprotected sex.

Instead of enabling your kids to lie and get away with it, put a swift and immediate end to any attempts to tell a lie.

If you let the little lies slide, you'll eventually find out you're being lied to about everything—and you'll have a heck of a time stopping it. Once a child or teenager gets in the habit of lying, it's a difficult habit to break. They'll lie to you about where they're going, who they're hanging out with and what they're doing when they're out with their friends.

As parents, we're the biggest role models our kids have. It's up to us to set a proper example for them. We can't lie, cheat and steal and then expect our kids not to follow in our footsteps. Lying to other people in front of your kids shows them you think it's OK. It doesn't matter that you've told them it isn't acceptable to lie; it's what you do when the cards are on the table that counts.

When your kids do lie, your first instinct is going to be to get angry at them and accuse them of hurting you. Lies are hurtful by nature and you want to let your children know they've broken your trust. The problem with taking this tact is your kids are now going to feel like bad people. They're not going to associate the lie with being bad and avoid lying because of it. They're going to associate being bad with you getting angry and will be more likely to lie next time.

When lying becomes an easy way out to avoid making you mad, guess what your kids are going to do? They're going to lie, lie and then lie some more to try to avoid making you angry.

So what can you do? The following tips can be used to help you raise (somewhat) honest kids:

- **Do set a good example yourself by not lying in front of your kids.**

- **Don't scream and yell when your kids do something wrong.** It will encourage them to lie because they aren't going to want to incur your wrath.
- **Don't allow your kids to get away with little lies.** They'll eventually turn into bigger lies.
- **Don't take lies personally.** Your kids aren't lying to you to hurt your feelings. Sure, lies are hurtful, but that isn't the intent when your kids tell you a lie.
- **Do remember that you aren't the only influence of your kids, but you are the biggest one.** Your kids are influenced by their environment. Even if you don't lie at home, they're going to be exposed to lies on television, at school and in print. It's up to you to steer them in the right direction.
- **Do set boundaries and lay out clear consequences for lying.**
- **Don't give up in the face of adversity. Kids will try to push you over the edge.** When your kid pushes his or her boundaries, don't budge. Push back and let them know their behavior isn't acceptable and won't be tolerated.
- **Don't make honesty the thing that determines whether or not your children are good people.** If you're constantly telling your kid what a bad person they are for lying, they're probably going to start living up to that expectation in other areas of their life. Let them know lies aren't acceptable, but don't beat what a bad person they are for lying into their head.

- **Do remember that even good kids lie sometimes.** As a parent, it's our job to make sure those lies don't get out of control. Good kids stay good kids with proper guidance.
- **Do separate the punishment for lying about an incident from the punishment for the incident itself.** If there is no separate consequence for lying, there's no reason not to lie the next time around. For example, if your teenage boy sneaks out at night and then lies about it in the morning, there needs to be a separate punishment handed down for the sneaking out and for lying about it. If you ground him for two weeks for sneaking out, you can add on taking away his cell phone and video games for lying about it. This sets clear and separate consequences for the action and for lying about the action. The next time he's caught red-handed, he'll think twice about lying about it because he knows the punishment will be more severe.

Chapter 11: Exposing Lies

"I'm not upset that you lied to me, I'm upset that from now on I can't believe you."

—Friedrich Nietzsche

Figuring out when someone is lying is only half the battle.

Exposing the lie, or lies, is the tougher half of the equation. The techniques laid out thus far in the book will give you a pretty good idea of when someone is lying. What they don't give you is the ability to expose that liar to the world. You aren't going to be able to call out a liar by telling the world you know they're lying because they looked to the left while recalling details and their micro-expressions and body language told you they were lying.

You're going to need more evidence than body language and verbal cues. You're going to need either a confession or enough evidence to prove the person telling the lies wrong.

Lies about factual information are easy to prove wrong. All you need is a reliable source of information that unequivocally proves the stated information is incorrect. If you have a cell phone with Internet access, you can look the information up on the spot. When it comes to sales meetings and presentations, you can arm yourself with the knowledge you need in advance. Research the product you're being sold and print out the relevant information. A printed spec sheet from the manufacturer may be all you need to prove an unscrupulous salesman wrong.

If the person continues to insist they're right even when shown printed information that says otherwise, ask them to put what they're telling you in writing. This will give you something to fall back on later on down the road if the information you've been given turns out to be incorrect.

Fabrications about events and incidents are harder to disprove. There is no reliable printed source of information that you can fall back on to tell whether a story is true or not.

You can interview witnesses to try to piece the story together, but that isn't always reliable. Witnesses can be coerced into making false statements or they may skew a story so it favors a friend or family member. It's also possible they don't remember the story and are creating memories to fill in the blanks.

If there's any doubt as to the veracity of witness statements, ask any police officer who's had to interview multiple witnesses of a crime. Witnesses are notoriously unreliable. One witness may say the perpetrator was a tall, white mall with a wiry build, while the other will say the perp was definitely a short Hispanic man with a mustache. Neither witness is intentionally lying, but their memories of the event are completely different.

Verifying a story by interviewing those involved can help you piece together what happened, but it doesn't always give you an accurate picture of what actually happened. If you have widely varying accounts of an event, the truth usually lies somewhere in the middle.

When you're talking to someone who is telling a story or recalling events that you suspect are fabricated, watch for inconsistencies in the story. A person who tells you they were on the scene of a crime and heard screams but didn't witness what happened is probably lying. Humans are curious by nature and their first instinct is to look and see what's going on.

When you find an inconsistency in the story, start asking pointed questions about it and try to get the person to slip up. An inexperience liar will get flustered when they realize they're about to get caught and may slip up and make even more glaring mistakes with their logic.

Sometimes it helps to let something go for a while before you come back to it. Wait until the person is comfortably lying and then hit them with the inconsistency. Tell them you're wondering about something, and then ask them about the error in logic they just made. Ask for specific details and try to make them slip up with the little stuff. The more details you ask for now, the more the person lying is going to have to try to keep straight in their head.

A person who is telling the truth probably isn't going to be able to recall all of the minor details of a situation. A person who is lying will make up details as he goes because he wants it to appear that he vividly remembers the event. Keep on asking for tiny details until they've built up to the point where the person is having trouble keeping them straight and then go back to some of the earlier details and ask pointed questions about them. Unless the person has a photographic memory, they aren't going to be able to keep all of the details straight.

Another item liars have trouble with is keeping the chronological order of the stories they're telling straight. They'll tell the story from beginning to end, but will have trouble jumping around in the chronology. Try asking a question about a sequence of events in the beginning of the story and then jump to the end and ask about a sequence of events. If the story isn't true, the person is going to have trouble jumping around like that.

The more information a liar gives, the more likely they are to slip up. The key to keeping information flowing is to make them comfortable. Ask questions in a calm, relaxed manner and don't make it seem as if the person is being interrogated. Friendly banter reveals a lot more about a person than angry interrogation.

Be aware that there are a small percentage of people who are able to fool even the experts. They usually aren't versed in the art of lying; they're simply innately good at pulling the wool over people's eyes. You may suspect a person like this is lying, but never be able to get enough information to actually prove the person is telling a lie. In this case, it's better off to just distance yourself from the person and leave the lies alone. A liar that's good at lying can make your life a living hell if they think you're onto them.